The Ten Pillars of Buddhism

Sangharakshita

The Ten Pillars of Buddhism

Sangharakshita

Windhorse Publications

Published by
Windhorse Publications Ltd.
169 Mill Road
Cambridge
CB1 3AN, UK
info@windhorsepublications.com
www.windhorsepublications.com

© Sangharakshita 1984

First published 1984
Second edition 1985, third edition 1989, fourth edition
1996, this edition 2010

The right of Sangharakshita to be identified as the author
of this work has been asserted by him in accordance with
the Copyright, Designs and Patents Act 1988

Cover design by Stefanie Ine Grewe. Initial concept by
Peter Wenman.
Author photograph by Alokavira/Timm Sonnenschein,
www.timmsonnenschein.com
Printed by Bell & Bain Ltd., Glasgow

British Library Cataloguing in Publication Data:
A catalogue record for this book is available from the
British Library

ISBN: 9781 907314 01 8
ISSN: 2042-0560

Mixed Sources
Product group from well-managed
forests and other controlled sources
www.fsc.org Cert no. TT-COC-002769
© 1996 Forest Stewardship Council
FSC

Contents

Foreword

As the opening passage of this book makes clear, the paper reproduced here was first delivered to a gathering of members of the Western Buddhist Order (now known as the Triratna Buddhist Order), in London, in April 1984. The occasion marked the celebration of the Order's sixteenth anniversary, and the theme of the paper was one of fundamental importance to all those present: the Ten Precepts. These Precepts are the ten ethical principles that Order members 'receive' at the time of their ordination, and which they undertake subsequently to observe as a spiritually potent aspect of their everyday lives.

The theme was therefore a very basic and seemingly down-to-earth one, but here, as he is wont to do, Sangharakshita demonstrated that no theme is so 'basic' that it can be taken for granted. As a communication from the Enlightened mind, the various formulations and expressions of the Buddha's teaching can be turned to again and again; their freshness and relevance can never be exhausted.

As he spoke, it was clear that Sangharakshita was addressing a far larger audience than that which was present at the time. The relevance of his material extended of course to those Order members, present and future, who could not be there on that occasion. But it reached out further than that, to the entire, wider 'Buddhist world', and still further, to all those who, whether Buddhist or not, seek guidance and insights in their quest for ethical standards by which to live.

In the hope, therefore, that it will reach at least some more members of that vast audience, we are very happy to publish that paper in the form of this book.

Perhaps the central point to emerge in Part 1, where Sangharakshita is addressing himself to a more decidedly Buddhist audience, is that the list of Ten Precepts being examined is not to be regarded as simply one more list – and a rather short one at that – among the many other lists. It is qualitatively different. It is a list that addresses itself to acts of body, speech, and mind, thus providing a formula that has reference to the whole being of man.

Other traditional lists, most of which are much longer, may indeed work out and emphasize certain matters of detail that fall within their scope, but none of them offer the same comprehensiveness. Because of this unique comprehensiveness, the Ten Precepts can be said to contain a fundamental set of ethical principles for the spiritual life: a *Mula-Pratimoksa*.

In expounding this set of precepts, Sangharakshita is offering for the consideration of the entire Buddhist Sangha a formula for ethical life that cuts through the layers of often lifeless formalism and legalistic detail that have not only sapped the life from other formulations, but which have also been used all too often as agents in the disunification of the Buddhist Spiritual Community.

This offer is made along with the plea that the precepts – in no matter what formulation – should never be regarded as more than expressions of what is in fact the highest common factor of Buddhism: the Going for Refuge. It is only out of a fundamental commitment to higher levels of being that higher values, and therefore ethical precepts, can evolve.

In this section Sangharakshita is therefore offering to all schools and sects of the Buddhist Sangha a key to unity, a key to the experience of 'Mahasangha'. Those who assume that such a key could only be turned at the price of a weakening of spiritual commitment and integrity may be heartened to find that the precise opposite is the case.

Western Buddhists, Eastern Buddhists, and non-Buddhists alike will find a wealth of day-to-day, practical value in Part 2. Here, Sangharakshita explores each of the Ten Precepts in turn, asking us to turn the lens of moral vision onto one aspect of our lives after another. Dwelling as much on their 'positive' formulations as on the more often quoted 'negative' ones, he helps us to discover the precepts for what they are: not dry rules, but challenging reflexes of a genuine commitment to the spiritual life and spiritual values. As we follow him along the way we may be surprised to find ourselves surrounded, not by walls, fences, and narrow tracks, but by ten great pillars, each one brilliant and sparkling with precious stones and gems, together supporting the sky-like majesty of the spiritual life.

Nagabodhi

Sukhavati, 20 June 1984

Foreword to the Fifth Edition

This paper was given by Sangharakshita in 1984, well before I first stepped through the doors of the Buddhist Centre in East London, where I learned to meditate in 1990. Now, 19 years later, I am working at Tiratanaloka, where we offer retreats for women who are training to enter the Triratna Buddhist Order. We run a retreat on Buddhist ethics as part of this process, where we study this text in depth.

This list of the 'ten principles of ethics' was first set out 2,500 years ago by the Buddha. In the modern world we can read this as a fairly standard list of dos and don'ts, and rapidly move on to more exciting teachings about emptiness or Bodhicitta. However, Sangharakshita reminds us here that ethics is deeply relevant to practising Buddhists; studying and discussing it with women of all ages and nationalities has given me a profound sense of gratitude for the clarity and wisdom of his elucidation of this very important teaching of the Buddha.

Sangharakshita gave this paper on the sixteenth anniversary of the Western Buddhist Order (now the Triratna Buddhist Order), and described it then as the movement reaching its collective majority. Reaching adulthood is seen as the time when we are able to take ethical responsibility, when we are 'grown up' enough to understand the effect we have on other people, and to take responsibility for that. It is the point when we can be tried and jailed for criminal offences; or, for that matter, decide to get married.

Before I was Buddhist I thought of moral codes as ways of governing the ongoing battle between my ego and the rest of society. What would I do if I could do it with impunity? Do I ever really want to be good? I used to imagine that there would always be a tension between what I want and what others want me to be or do. This conflict of egos had to be balanced by more or less arbitrary notions of fairness, and policed with rewards and punishments. My involvement in politics was, at bottom, concerned with where we draw the lines of power, and how we police them.

It has been an enormously important stage in my own personal 'growing up' to realise that Buddhist ethics aren't like this; they are based on love. The extraordinary 'wisdom of the gentle Buddhas' tells us that ultimately there can be no conflict between myself and others; that in working to benefit others I benefit myself most fully; and that if I abandon even one other being, I am damaging myself.

Sangharakshita says: 'A lot of people nowadays are convinced (as regards ethics) of two principles: if it doesn't hurt anybody it can't be wrong, and if you're not found out it doesn't really matter.' Our modern

Western culture has strong nihilistic tendencies; consumerism means that we are valued according to our possessions and status, with the subtext that therefore human life in itself is valueless. The Judaeo-Christian model of competitive goodness and fear of punishment means that we need to find the 'culprit' to blame when something goes wrong. Then there is relativism, the idea that there are no absolute moral truths, each cultural form having its own internal validity; and the pervading cynicism of today which refuses to believe that anything more than self-interest really motivates anyone.

The basic Buddhist insight is that what we call 'me' is actually a constantly changing pattern, and that we can, by our conscious choices, affect this flow. The law of karma can be looked at as a 'feedback loop' by which our present actions (whether of body, speech or mind) affect what we become in the future. This means that as Buddhists we are in training: in this sense it is an ethics of 'training principles'. By working at changing our mental states – the intentions and views that drive our actions – we are consciously moving from what Sangharakshita has called the 'reactive' to the 'creative' mind.

However, the ten precepts outlined by the Buddha go a step further than being a method of becoming better and happier people; they offer us the way into an altogether different attitude to existence. In this book Sangharakshita unfolds his vision of the 'power mode' and 'love mode' as two different ways of living, and the Buddhist path as one of making a comprehensive shift from one to the other. In the power mode we are trying to control the world to suit our desires, whereas the love mode consists in consciously cultivating a relationship of appreciative solidarity with it. Sangharakshita calls this a 'cherishing, protecting, maturing love, that has the same kind of effect on the spiritual being of others as the light and heat of the sun have on their physical being.' So we are aiming to transform both ourselves, and our relationship to the world and to other people, at the same time.

In the modern world this message is of huge importance, and has a number of consequences that can look quite different from the expressions of conventional morality we are used to. These are some of the issues that have emerged for me as I've studied this text with women who have asked for ordination.

Most importantly, this is an 'ethics of intention': it is our intentions that make a difference in this process of transformation, and I can make the choice at every moment to let my mind work with the grain of reality rather than against it – this is what is meant by a 'skilful' act. There are no private moments in this ethics: whether I am seen or not, I still have to train myself; and there's no point in being seen to be 'in the right'. In fact, defending or hiding my worse actions is meaningless, as I am the one who really wants to change the mental states that drive them, and by disclosing them to my friends I can get clarity about motivations that are hidden to me, and even discover blind spots.

Ultimately, the practice of this ethics has an unconditional quality: it cannot be a sort of reciprocity or bargaining – where I'll only clean the dishes if I see you do your share. Even if I find myself, by no fault of my own, in a tough position, that does not mean that I am therefore 'justified' in acting unskilfully.

Only I can tell what the intentions are behind my actions, speech and thoughts. I have to be aware of these motivations, and try to integrate them around my ideals and values.

This obviously means that we have to be very careful in judging other people's ethics. As these are principles rather than rules, we will each be working on them to differing degrees at different times in our lives, and while we may question another person's actions we can never fully know their intentions. We normally feel that it is important that everyone acts in accord with a single moral code, legally enforced; however, Buddhist ethics is more individual, and each of us must take personal responsibility for the effect our actions have on the world and on ourselves. In fact, this ethics can never be about punishing people, since we are training ourselves to respond to others with compassion. So, although I may have to use power to restrain someone if they are damaging themselves or others, it must always be from a basis of love. Sangharakshita says: 'Whenever one has to operate in accordance with the power mode, the power mode must always be subordinated to the love mode.' This would mean that even in cases where I have been hurt by someone, ideally I care about what happens to them as much as I care about myself

However, our actions also have an effect on our intentions, and this ethics can involve acting as if we already had a level of Enlightenment. Thus the ethical precepts followed by Buddhists are based on the way an Enlightened person would naturally act, and by carrying them out we find out how Enlightenment might feel. This is quite a subtle point – since 'acting as if' clearly exposes us to the danger of hypocrisy, it needs to be linked to a high level of awareness of our motivation, and honesty about ourselves.

Using ethics in this way is a radical departure from a Christian or social ethics, where we simply protect others from our inherent bad tendencies. Instead, ethical action becomes a transformative practice; becomes in fact the 'process of spiritual life and growth' itself. In his *Survey of Buddhism* Sangharakshita compares the practice of ethics with reading a poem: whereas the poet passes from intensely felt emotion to its embodiment in a poem, the reader passes from the words of the poem to the feelings by which it was inspired. 'Morality is, as it were, the words of that most perfect of all poems, the holy life, the language which makes intelligible the secrets of spirituality.'

Changing greed, hatred and delusion into generosity, compassion and wisdom, though a very high ideal, is one I find very attractive. The Buddha is saying that through ethical practice we can 'purify the heart', and with a pure heart we will be able to see things as they really are: we will see reality as blissful, vivid and open. In fact, the creative mind is deeply satisfying; living in the love mode is far more enjoyable than the constant battle of the power mode relationship with the world. One of the best-known quotes from the Buddha's teaching is from the *Dhammapada*, where the Buddha says: 'For hatred does not cease by hatred at any time: hatred ceases by love, this is an old rule. The world does not know that we must all come to an end here; but those who know it, their quarrels cease at once.'

Vajrasakhi

Tiratanaloka, December 2009

About the Author

Sangharakshita was born Dennis Lingwood in South London, in 1925. Largely self-educated, he developed an interest in the cultures and philosophies of the East early on, and realized that he was a Buddhist at the age of sixteen.

The Second World War took him, as a conscript, to India, where he stayed on to become the Buddhist monk Sangharakshita ('protector of the spiritual community'). After studying for some years under leading teachers from the major Buddhist traditions, he went on to teach and write extensively. He also played a key part in the revival of Buddhism in India, particularly through his work among the 'ex-Untouchables'.

After twenty years in India he returned to England to establish the Friends of the Western Buddhist Order (FWBO) in 1967, and the Western Buddhist Order (called Trailokya Bauddha Mahasangha in India) in 1968. A translator between East and West, between the traditional world and the modern, between principles and practices, Sangharakshita's depth of experience and clear thinking have been appreciated throughout the world. He has always particularly emphasized the decisive significance of commitment in the spiritual life, the paramount value of spiritual friendship and community, the link between religion and art, and the need for a 'new society' supportive of spiritual aspirations and ideals.

In 2010 the FWBO was given a new name – the Triratna Buddhist Community – and the Order was renamed the Triratna Buddhist Order. The Triratna Buddhist Community is now an international Buddhist movement, with centres in many countries worldwide. In recent years Sangharakshita has been handing over most of his responsibilities to his senior disciples in the Order. From his base in Birmingham, UK, he now focuses on personal contact with people, though he still visits as many of the movement's centres as he can.

The Ten Precepts

I undertake the item of training which consists in abstention from killing living beings.

I undertake the item of training which consists in abstention from taking the not-given.

I undertake the item of training which consists in abstention from sexual misconduct.

I undertake the item of training which consists in abstention from false speech.

I undertake the item of training which consists in abstention from harsh speech.

I undertake the item of training which consists in abstention from frivolous speech.

I undertake the item of training which consists in abstention from slanderous speech.

I undertake the item of training which consists in abstention from covetousness.

I undertake the item of training which consists in abstention from hatred.

I undertake the item of training which consists in abstention from false views.

The Ten Positive Precepts

With deeds of loving-kindness
I purify my body.

With open-handed generosity
I purify my body.

With stillness, simplicity, and contentment
I purify my body.

With truthful communication
I purify my speech.

With words kindly and gracious
I purify my speech.

With utterance helpful and harmonious
I purify my speech.

Abandoning covetousness for tranquillity
I purify my mind.

Changing hatred into compassion
I purify my mind.

Transforming ignorance into wisdom
I purify my mind.

Introduction

The Western Buddhist Order (known in India as the Trailokya Bauddha Mahasangha) was founded in London in 1968. Today we meet to celebrate its sixteenth anniversary – or sixteenth birthday, as one might say. Without being over fanciful one might, perhaps, attach a special significance to the fact that the Order has now attained this particular number of years. Sixteen is twice eight, or four times four, and both four and eight are traditionally regarded as numbers indicative of 'squareness' and stability. It is also the sum of ten and six, both of which numbers have their own symbolical associations. In pre-Buddhist Indian tradition groups of sixteen, or sixteenfold divisions of things, are extremely common. One of the commonest is that of the sixteen 'digits' of the moon. Sixteenth parts are also referred to in Buddhist literature. Thus in the *Itivuttaka* the Buddha declares:

> Monks, whatsoever grounds there be for good works undertaken with a view to rebirth, all of them are not worth one sixteenth part of that goodwill [i.e. *metta*] which is the heart's

1

release; goodwill alone, which is the heart's release, shines and burns and flashes forth in surpassing them. Just as, monks, the radiance of all the starry bodies is not worth one sixteenth part of the moon's radiance, but the moon's radiance shines and burns and flashes forth, even so, monks, goodwill ... flashes forth in surpassing good works undertaken with a view to rebirth.[1]

Perhaps the best-known group of sixteen in Buddhism is that of the sixteen Arhants – mysterious personages who exist from age to age and periodically reinvigorate the Sasana.

For many people in the FWBO, however, whether Order members, Mitras, or Friends, the most familiar association of the figure sixteen – the one that springs most readily to mind – is with the 'archetypal' Bodhisattvas. Manjusri, Avalokitesvara, and the rest, are all described in the literature, and depicted in the visual arts, of Buddhism, as appearing in the surpassingly beautiful form of Indian princes, clad in rich silks and adorned with jewels, and *sixteen years old*. They are sixteen because sixteen is the age at which a youth is considered, in India, to have attained to the full development of his faculties, both physical and mental, to be in the full bloom of masculine strength and beauty, and to be ready for the duties and responsibilities of adult life. In Western terms, at sixteen one reaches the years of discretion, one grows up, one passes from immaturity to maturity. The sixteenth birthday therefore has, for Indian tradition, something of the significance that the twenty-first birthday has in the West, the five-year difference between them no doubt being attributable to the fact that in Europe and North America human beings mature later than they do in warmer climes.

In celebrating its sixteenth birthday the Order is therefore celebrating, i.e. we as Order members are celebrating, the attainment of our 'collective' majority as a Spiritual Community. We have reached the age of discretion. We have grown up. We have passed – collectively, at least – from immaturity to maturity. We now have our own front door key, and are free to come and go as we please. In celebrating the attainment of our majority, however, we must not forget that although we are Buddhists we are, most of us, also Westerners, and that it *may* take us a few more years to achieve, as an Order, the kind of spiritual maturity that is symbolized by the physical and mental maturity of the sixteen-year-old Indian youth. It may not be until our twenty-first birthday that the Order will, in fact, be a recognizable reflection, on the mundane level, of the thousand-armed and thousand-eyed sixteen-year-old Avalokitesvara.

Nonetheless, today is our sixteenth birthday, and therefore the day on which we celebrate the attainment of our 'official' majority, even though we may be a bit backward in our development. It was for this reason, partly, that I decided not only that as many of us should meet together on this occasion as possible but also that I should, as part of the proceedings, deliver a lecture or read a paper. It is not often that we are able to come together in this way. Most Order members are very busy, and there are problems of travel and accommodation, but it is at least some consolation that so large a section of the Order should have been able to gather here today – the more especially since we are not able to hold our biennial Convention this year as planned. The first of the seven times seven, minus one, conditions of the stability of the Order laid down by the Buddha shortly before his *parinirvana*, i.e. that the brethren should assemble repeatedly and in large numbers, is being fulfilled at least to a limited extent! Moreover, in gathering here today we do not forget those members of the Order who are unable to be with us and who, no doubt, are also celebrating our sixteenth birthday. We know that we are united with them, as they with us, through our common commitment to the Three Jewels, and through the all-pervading spirit of *metta* which, transcending time and space, links mind to mind and heart to heart in worldwide spiritual fellowship.

Now as soon as I had decided that I would give a lecture or read a paper to you today, I let it be known that I was open to suggestions as to what the subject of the lecture or paper should be. Various suggestions have, in fact, been made. They range from a suggestion that I should speak on whether there was a philosophical term or phrase that would summarize the nature of Buddhism, much as the term 'monotheism' summarizes the nature of Christianity and Islam, to the suggestion that I should speak on *prajna* in the sense of 'not settling down' – a sense which, according to the Order member making the suggestion, runs through the *Heart Sutra*.

However, I shall not be speaking on any of the topics suggested, though I hope to be able to say something about all of them, in one context or another, sooner or later. Since I do not often have the opportunity of personally addressing so many of you at the same time, I wanted to speak, on this our sixteenth birthday, on a topic of fundamental importance to the whole Order. After giving the matter some thought I therefore decided to speak on the Ten Precepts, i.e. the ten *akusala-dharmas* from which one undertakes to refrain, and the ten *kusala-dharmas* which one undertakes to observe, on the occasion of one's 'ordination' into the Western Buddhist Order or Trailokya Bauddha Mahasangha.

I have chosen this topic mainly for three reasons. Firstly, because despite the importance of the subject I have not – to the best of my recollection – ever devoted a whole lecture to it. Secondly, because as the years go by I see, more and more clearly, how profound is the significance, and how far-reaching the implications – both theoretical and practical – of each apparently simple precept. Thirdly, because I want to emphasize yet again our principle of 'more and more of less and less'– that is, our principle of trying to go more and more deeply into the so-called basic teachings of Buddhism rather than trying to hurry on to teachings which are allegedly more advanced. This emphasis is perhaps all the more necessary now that we are celebrating our sixteenth birthday. As I mentioned earlier, now that we are sixteen we have attained the years of discretion. We are grown up. But as I also mentioned, we may not, in fact, as an Order, be quite so mature as our sixteen years might lead us to suppose. One of the signs of immaturity – whether individual or collective – is that one thinks that now one is out of leading-strings, so to speak, one can safely forget the lessons learned in one's childhood. Translated into more specifically Buddhist terms, it means that one thinks one can afford to neglect the 'elementary' teachings of Buddhism – and by elementary one of course usually means the ethical teachings as embodied in, for example, the Five or the Eight or the Ten Precepts. It is in order to forestall any such development, rather than because I see any sign of it actually happening, that I want to speak on the Ten Precepts on this occasion.

I hope no one feels disappointed. I hope no one was expecting me to speak on some very advanced, or very esoteric, subject. If this was the case, and especially if anyone still harbours the idea that ethics is a dull and uninteresting topic, you will at least be glad to know that I am entitling this paper not simply 'The Ten Precepts', which admittedly does not sound very colourful or very inspiring, but 'The Ten Pillars of Buddhism'. The Ten Precepts are, indeed, the massy supports of the entire majestic edifice of the Dharma. Without the Ten Precepts the Dharma could not, in fact, exist. Continuing the architectural metaphor, one might say that the Three Jewels are the three-stepped plinth and foundation of the Dharma, the Ten Precepts the double row of pillars supporting the spacious dome, Meditation the dome itself, and Wisdom the lofty spire that surmounts the dome. Elaborating, one might say that each of the ten pillars was made of a precious stone or precious metal, so that there was a pillar of diamond, a pillar of gold, a pillar of crystal, and so on. In this way we would be able to gain not only an understanding of the importance of the Ten Precepts but also, perhaps, an appreciation of their splendour and beauty. Having exclaimed 'How charming is divine Philosophy', Milton, in a well-known passage, goes on to assert that it is

Not harsh and crabbéd as dull fools suppose
But musical as is Apollo's lute.

In similar vein one could assert that, like Buddhism itself, the subject of Buddhist ethics – particularly as represented by the Ten Precepts – was not dull and uninteresting, as to the superficial observer it might appear, but on the contrary full of light, life, warmth, and colour. Paraphrasing the paradoxical words of another poet, one might also say of Buddhist ethics – might say of the Ten Precepts – that you must love them before they will seem to you worthy of your love.

Though I may not have devoted a whole lecture to the subject of the Ten Precepts, I have certainly both spoken and written on Buddhist ethics, particularly as a constituent of the Noble Eightfold Path and of the Path of the Ten Paramitas or Perfections.[2] I have also dealt with the subject in an article entitled 'Aspects of Buddhist Morality', in which I discuss (1) The Nature of Morality, (2) Morality and the Spiritual Ideal, (3) Morality Mundane and Transcendental, (4) Patterns of Morality, (5) The Benefits of Morality, and (6) Determinants of Morality.[3] In the present paper I shall try to avoid covering ground I have already covered elsewhere, or dealing with matters that have been adequately dealt with by other writers on Buddhism, whether ancient or modern. In particular I shall try to avoid losing myself in the details of scholastic analysis in the sort of way that has become traditional for some forms of Buddhism.

Even limiting myself in this way there is still, however, a good deal of ground to be covered, and if I am to cover it even cursorily the subject-matter of this paper will have to be tightly organized. In speaking on 'The Ten Pillars of Buddhism' I shall therefore divide the paper into two parts. In the first part I shall deal with the Ten Precepts collectively, so to speak. In the second part I shall deal with them individually, i.e. I shall deal with each of the Ten Precepts separately. For the sake of further convenience, the discussion of the Ten Precepts collectively will be broken down into a discussion of eight distinct topics, between which there will of course be various interrelations and even a certain amount of overlapping. The eight topics are: (1) The Relation Between Refuges and Precepts, (2) The Canonical Sources of the Ten Precepts, (3) The Ten Precepts and Total Transformation, (4) The Ten Precepts as Principles of Ethics, (5) The Ten Precepts as Rules of Training, (6) The Ten Precepts as '*Mula-Pratimoksa*', (7) The Ten Precepts and Other Ethical Formulae, and (8) The Ten Precepts and Lifestyle. The division of the first part of the paper in this way will, I hope, enable us to obtain a more comprehensive view of the Ten Pillars of Buddhism in their collective majesty.

Part One

The Ten Precepts Collectively

1

The Relation Between Refuges and Precepts

The Three Refuges (or the Three Jewels) are, of course, the Buddha or Enlightened One, the Dharma or Teaching of the Way to Enlightenment, and the Sangha or Spiritual Community of those following the Way to Enlightenment, especially those who have attained to the higher, transcendental stages of spiritual progress from which recession is not possible. One goes for Refuge to the Buddha, the Dharma, and the Sangha – or, in more contemporary idiom, commits oneself to them – when one decides that to attain Enlightenment is the most important thing in human life, and when one acts – or does one's best to act – in accordance with that decision. This means organizing one's entire life, in all its different aspects, in such a way as to subserve the attainment of Enlightenment. It means placing the Ideal of Enlightenment, i.e. placing the Buddha (which Buddha one can oneself become) at the centre of one's personal Mandala, and arranging one's different interests and activities in such a way that they are placed nearer to, or further away from, the centre of that Mandala in accordance with the degree to which they help or hinder the attainment of Enlightenment. Interests and activities that are opposed to the Ideal of Enlightenment should, of course, be banished from the Mandala. Going for Refuge is the fundamental Buddhist act. It is what makes one a Buddhist, a follower of the Dharma, or a Dharmacari(ni). It is what makes one a member of the Sangha. The Going for Refuge is what, above all else, one has in common with other Buddhists. In other words, the Going for Refuge is the highest common factor of Buddhism.

Unfortunately, in many parts of the Buddhist world the Going for Refuge has long been regarded as the lowest common denominator of Buddhism rather than as the highest common factor – an undervaluation which was one of the main reasons behind the formation of the Western Buddhist Order. If there is any lowest common denominator in Buddhism it is, one might say, the Five, or the Eight, or the Ten Precepts which, on ceremonial occasions, one 'takes' from one's preceptor immediately after Going for Refuge. Again unfortunately, it is the observance of these Five, or Eight, or Ten Precepts, rather than the threefold Going for Refuge, that has come to be regarded as the highest common factor – instead of as the lowest common denominator – of Buddhism, with the result that the Buddhist community has tended to be divided by the fact that some of its members observed a lesser, and some a greater, number of precepts (generally five in the case of the 'laity' and a total of 227 or 250 in the case of the 'monks'), rather than united by the fact that they all went for Refuge to the same Buddha, Dharma, and Sangha.[4]

Without understanding the supreme importance of the Going for Refuge as the central act of the Buddhist life it is quite impossible to understand the true nature of the relation between the Refuges and the Precepts. This principle holds good regardless of the actual number of precepts one undertakes to observe. The relation between Refuges and Precepts is not merely external. It is not that having gone for Refuge to the Buddha, the Dharma, and the Sangha, one now undertakes, in addition to that, to observe the Five, or the Eight, or the Ten, or any other particular number of Precepts. It is not that when, on ceremonial occasions, one recites first the Going-for-Refuge formula and then, immediately afterwards, the Precept-acceptance formula, one recites them in this order for purely historical reasons, so to speak, and that had things turned out differently one might just as well have been reciting them in the reverse order. The relation between one's Going for Refuge and one's observance of the Precepts is an organic one, observance of the Precepts being as much an expression of Going for Refuge as the flower is an expression of the seed or his *nuvre* an expression of the writer or artist. In a sense, the Going for Refuge and the observance of the Precepts are part of a single process of spiritual life and growth.

When one places the Buddha, that is to say places the Spiritual Ideal, at the centre of one's personal Mandala, a radical reorganization of the contents of that Mandala naturally follows. If no such reorganization follows, then one's placing of the Buddha at the centre of one's Mandala has been purely nominal, or perhaps what one has placed there is not really the Buddha at all. The placing of the Buddha at the centre of one's personal Mandala corresponds to Going for Refuge. The radical reorganization of the contents of that Mandala corresponds to the observance of the Precepts as its natural consequence, that is to say, as the prolongation of the act of Going for Refuge itself into every aspect of one's existence.

Going for Refuge, or commitment to the Three Jewels, is one's life-blood as a Buddhist. Observance of the Precepts represents the circulation of that blood through every fibre of one's being. By its very nature blood must circulate. If it does not circulate this means that the organism to which it belongs is dead, and that the blood itself, stagnating, will soon cease to be blood. Similarly, by its very nature the Going for Refuge must find expression in the observance of the Precepts. If it does not find such expression this means that as a Buddhist one is virtually dead and that the Going for Refuge itself, becoming more and more mechanical, will soon cease to be effectively such.

It is because the Going for Refuge must find expression in the total transformation of the individual, both in himself (or herself) and in his or her relations with other people, and because this total transformation is represented more adequately by the Ten Precepts than by any other set of precepts, that in the Western Buddhist Order (Triratna Buddhist Community) we not only go for Refuge to the Buddha, the Dharma, and the Sangha, but also undertake to observe the *Ten* Precepts rather than the Five, or the Eight, or any other specific number of precepts. To the topic of the Ten Precepts and Total Transformation we must now therefore turn. Before we do so, however, let me briefly remind you of what I have called the Canonical Sources of the Ten Precepts. Buddhist friends outside the FWBO have been known to doubt whether the Ten Precepts observed by members of the Western Buddhist Order were actually taught by the Buddha, and whether they are anywhere to be found in the Buddhist scriptures, and it therefore behoves us to be sure of our ground.

2

The Canonical Sources of the Ten Precepts

It is well known that the Buddha wrote nothing, and that for several generations his teachings were preserved by purely oral means. Only when the orally transmitted traditions were finally written down did there come into existence what we call the Buddhist scriptures or the canonical literature of Buddhism. Following the classification adopted during the period of oral transmission, this vast body of material was traditionally known as the Tripitaka or 'Three Collections', the three being the Vinaya Pitaka or Collection of Monastic Discipline, the Sutra Pitaka or Collection of Discourses, and the Abhidharma Pitaka or Collection of Further Doctrine. Both spiritually and historically speaking, the most important of the three is the Sutra Pitaka, and references to the Ten Precepts, in one form or another, are to be found in each of the four (or in the case of the Pali Tipitaka, five) *agamas* or *nikayas* of which this Pitaka consists.

In the case of the Pali recension of the Tripitaka, the first reference to the Ten Precepts is to be found in the *Kutadanta Sutta*, the fifth sutta of the *Digha-Nikaya* or 'Collection of Long Discourses'. This sutta deals with the subject of sacrifice, and is concerned to establish the superiority of the purely moral and spiritual 'sacrifice' taught by the Buddha over the bloody sacrifices of the old Brahminical religion. The brahmin Kutadanta, who gives his name to the title of the sutta, has assembled many hundreds of animals in readiness for a great sacrifice, but not knowing how to perform it, with its threefold method and its *sixteen* accessory instruments (another important instance of this numerical group), he decides to go and ask the Buddha, who knows all about such things. In response to Kutadanta's enquiry the Buddha relates the story of a great king of former times called Mahavijita. This king, too, had wanted to offer a great sacrifice, and had asked the royal chaplain to instruct him how the sacrifice should be performed. The royal chaplain (who, it turns out, was the Buddha himself in a previous existence) had thereupon given what was, in effect, a systematic allegorization of the entire sacrificial procedure. Among other things, he told the king – and it is with this part of the sutta that we are at present concerned – about the different kinds of men who would come to his sacrifice.

> Now there will come to your sacrifice, Sire, men who destroy the life of living things, and men who refrain therefrom – men who take

what has not been given, and men who refrain
therefrom – men who act evilly in respect of
lusts, and men who refrain therefrom – men
who speak lies, and men who do not – men
who slander, and men who do not – men who
speak rudely, and men who do not – men
who chatter vain things, and men who refrain
therefrom – men who covet, and men who
covet not – men who harbour ill-will, and
men who harbour it not – men whose views
are wrong, and men whose views are right.[5]

Here the Ten Precepts, in their positive and negative
forms, are clearly referred to. After being given
further instruction by the Buddha, who sets forth
for his benefit the successive stages of spiritual
progress, Kutadanta realizes what is the best sacrifice
of all and obtains the pure and spotless Eye of Truth,
thus becoming a Stream Entrant. The fact that the
Ten Precepts should be referred to, in this sutta, in
the context of a story of former times is interesting,
suggesting as it does that for the compilers of the
Collection of Long Discourses this particular ethical
formula was of great antiquity, or that it belonged, as
we would say, to the earliest days of Buddhism.

Passing from the *Digha-Nikaya* to the *Majjhima-
Nikaya* or 'Collection of Middle Length Discourses',
we find a detailed exposition of the Ten Precepts
in the important *Sevitabba-asevitabba-sutta*, or

'Discourse on What is to be Followed and What is Not to be Followed' (*Majjhima-Nikaya* no.114). The exposition is given not by the Buddha but by Sariputta, who explains to the monks what he understands to be the meaning in full of what has just been spoken by the Buddha in brief. There are two kinds of bodily conduct, the Buddha has told them, two kinds of vocal conduct, and two kinds of mental conduct, as well as two kinds of arising of thoughts, two kinds of assumption of perception, two kinds of assumption of views, and two kinds of assumption of individuality – and in the case of each dyad there is one kind which should be followed and one which should not be followed. Sariputta explains this by distinguishing between that kind of bodily conduct etc. as a result of which unskilled (*akusala*) states of mind grow much and skilled (*kusala*) states decrease, and that kind as a result of which unskilled states of mind decrease and skilled states of mind grow much. The first kind should not be followed, the second kind should be followed. Applying this to bodily conduct, vocal conduct, and mental conduct (the four other dyads appear to be treated as subdivisions of mental conduct), he describes in each case what kind of conduct makes unskilled states of mind grow and skilled states decrease, and vice versa. In this way he describes, in some detail, the ten *akusala-dhammas* from which a man should abstain, and the ten *kusala-dhammas* which he should observe and cultivate – that

21

is, he describes the Ten Precepts. (Significantly, it is only *bhikkhus* or 'monks' who are present throughout the sutta.)

As an example of Sariputta's exposition, all of which is approved and in fact repeated verbatim by the Buddha, let me quote part of his explanation of the content of the eighth and ninth Precepts, i.e. abstention from covetousness and from malevolence and the cultivation of their opposites. First, he is careful to make clear what it is he is explaining. In expositions of this sort we can, perhaps, see the beginnings of the Abhidharma, with which the name of Sariputta is, of course, associated.

'I, monks, say that mental conduct is of two kinds, one of which is to be followed and the other which is not to be followed; and there is this disparity in mental conduct.' This was said by the Lord. In reference to what was it said? Revered sir, if a certain kind of mental conduct is followed and unskilled states of mind grow much, skilled states of mind decrease, this kind of mental conduct is not to be followed.

And what kind of mental conduct, revered sir, does a man follow that unskilled states of mind grow much in him, skilled states of mind decrease? As to this, revered sir, someone is covetous; he covets that which is the property of another, thinking: 'O might that which is the other's be mine'; he is malevolent in thought, corrupt in mind and purpose, and thinks: 'Let these beings be killed or slaughtered or annihilated or destroyed, or may they not exist at all.' If this kind of mental conduct is followed, revered sir, unskilled states of mind grow much, skilled states of mind decrease.

And what kind of mental conduct, revered sir, does a man follow that unskilled states of mind decrease in him, skilled states of mind grow much? As to this, revered sir, someone is not covetous; he does not covet that which is the property of another, thinking: 'O might that which is the other's be mine'; he is not malevolent in thought, not corrupt in mind and purpose, but thinks: 'Let these beings, free from enmity, peaceable, secure and happy, look after self.' If this kind of mental conduct is followed, revered sir, unskilled states of mind decrease, skilled states of mind grow much. When the Lord said: 'I, monks, say that mental conduct is of two kinds, one of which is to be followed and the other of which is not to be followed; and there is this disparity in mental conduct,' it was said in reference to this.[6]

Though the *Sevitabba-asevitabba-sutta* is perhaps the most important of the Pali canonical sources of the Ten Precepts, there are a number of others also. In particular there is an important group of about fifty short suttas in the *Anguttara-Nikaya* or 'Collection of Gradual (or Numerical) Sayings', i.e. sayings on the ones, the twos, the threes, and so on up to the elevens. Many of these suttas differ only in respect of the place at which they were delivered, and the person to whom the teaching was addressed, the speaker being in all cases the Buddha himself. Some suttas resemble the *Kutadanta Sutta* in that the observance of the Ten Precepts is represented as being a better way of offering a sacrifice, or performing rites of purification, or making offerings to the dead. Among the suttas of this type there is one (untitled) sutta which is characteristic of the whole group. In this sutta the Buddha explains to Cunda the silversmith, who finds satisfaction in the purifying rites of 'the brahmins of the west who carry water-pots', in what real purification consists. After describing how the Ten Precepts are observed in their negative form, he proceeds to describe how they are observed in their positive form:

But, Cunda, threefold is cleansing by body, fourfold is cleansing by speech, threefold is cleansing by mind. And how is cleansing by body threefold?

Herein, Cunda, a certain one abandons taking life, abstains therefrom; he has laid aside the rod, has laid aside the knife; he dwells

24

modest, charitable, feeling compassion towards every living creature.

He abandons taking what is not given, abstains therefrom; the property of another, situated in jungle or in village, if not given, he takes not with thievish intent.

In sexual desires he abandons wrong action, abstains therefrom. He has no intercourse with girls in ward of mother or father, brother, sister or relatives (or clan), with girls lawfully guarded, already plighted to a husband and protected by the rod, even with girls crowned with the flower-garlands (of betrothal). Thus, Cunda, threefold is cleansing by body.

And how is cleansing by speech fourfold? Herein, Cunda, a certain one abandons lying, abstains therefrom. When cited to appear before the council or a company or amid his relatives or guild-men or before the royal family and asked to bear witness with the words: 'Come, good fellow! Say what you know,' not knowing, he says 'I know not'; knowing, he says 'I know'; not having seen, he says 'I saw not'; having seen, he says 'I saw'. Thus for his own sake or for the sake of others or to get some carnal profit or other he does not utter any deliberate falsehood.

Abandoning slanderous speech he abstains therefrom. When he hears something at one place he does not proclaim it elsewhere to bring about a quarrel between the parties: thus he brings together the discordant, restores harmony; harmony is his delight; he exults in, is passionately fond of harmony; he utters speech that makes for harmony. Also he abandons harsh speech, abstains therefrom. Whatsoever speech is blameless, pleasant to the ear, affectionate, going to the heart, urbane, agreeable to many folk, delightful to many folk, of such speech he is a speaker. Also abandoning idle babble he abstains therefrom; he speaks in season, of facts, of the aim, of Dhamma, of discipline; he utters speech worth treasuring up, speech seasonable and worth listening to, discriminating and concerned with the aim.

Thus, Cunda, fourfold is cleansing by speech. And how is cleansing by mind threefold?

Here a certain one is not covetous: he covets not the property of another, thinking: O that what is another's were mine! He is not malevolent of heart; the thoughts of his heart are not corrupt. He wishes: Let these beings carry about the self in peace, free from enmity, free from sorrow and in happiness.

Also he has right view: he is reasonable in outlook, holding that there are such things as gift, offering, oblation, fruit and ripening of deeds done well or ill; that this world is, that the world beyond is; that mother, father and beings of supernatural birth (in other worlds) do exist; that there are in the world recluses and brahmins who have gone rightly, who fare rightly, men who of their own comprehension have realized this world and the world beyond and thus declare it.

Thus, Cunda, threefold is the cleansing by the mind. So these are the ten ways of right doing.[7]

In other suttas the Buddha speaks of the observance and the non-observance of the Ten Precepts (usually in their negative form only) in terms of the hither and the farther shore, Dhamma and not-Dhamma, the bright and the dark way, and so on, thus making it clear that the Ten Precepts represent a pattern of ethical behaviour that can be looked at in a number of different ways, and from a number of different points of view. In several suttas, moreover, the Buddha speaks in terms of one's possessing or not possessing ten, or twenty, or thirty, or forty meritorious or demeritorious qualities. The ten qualities are equivalent to one's observing (or not observing) the Ten Precepts, the twenty qualities to one's not only observing (or not observing) them oneself, but also encouraging (or not encouraging) another to observe them too. Similarly, the thirty qualities consist in one's observing the Ten Precepts oneself, encouraging another to do likewise, and giving one's approval thereto (as well as the opposites of these), while the forty qualities are the thirty qualities plus speaking in praise, or not speaking in praise, of the Ten Precepts. Here the self-regarding and other-regarding aspects of the ethical and spiritual life are given equal prominence.

The canonical sources of the Ten Precepts are also to be found in the Sanskrit recension of the Tripitaka, including the Mahayana sutras. Since the fact that the Ten Precepts were actually taught by the Buddha, and are indeed to be found in the Buddhist scriptures, has already been sufficiently established, I shall deal with the Sanskrit canonical sources of the Ten Precepts even more summarily than with their Pali counterparts. The Sanskrit recension of the Tripitaka does not, of course, survive complete in the original language. Of the portions that do survive, one of the most interesting and important is the *Mahavastu*, a work which purports to belong to the Vinaya-Pitaka of the Lokuttaravadins, a sub-school of the Mahasanghikas, though it does not deal with Vinaya or monastic discipline in the ordinary sense of the term at all. The *Mahavastu* is, in fact, a highly devotional 'legendary biography' of the Buddha, interspersed with numerous Jatakas or Birth Stories. It is in one of the Jatakas that the reference to the Ten Precepts occurs.

The Jataka in question is the Kinnari Jataka, a charming tale of love, adventure, and magic that recalls the Arthurian romances and the stories of the *Arabian Nights Entertainments* rather than the sort of material normally found in the Buddhist scriptures, especially the Vinaya-Pitaka. There is no time even to summarize the Kinnari Jataka, but at one point Prince Sudhanu, who is the hero of the tale and, therefore, the Buddha himself in a previous existence, attends the great Brahminical sacrifice which King Sucandrima is about to perform 'with every kind of animal', including Manohara, the Kinnari or 'elf maiden', the heroine of the tale, who has just been captured. When Prince Sudhanu asks the King why so many living beings (including the unfortunate Kinnari) are enclosed in the sacrificial enclosure, and what profit there is in the sacrifice, the King replies that the living beings who will be slain in the sacrifice will go to heaven, while he himself will be reborn in heaven a number of times equal to the number of beings he will slay in the sacrifice.

The prince is deeply shocked, and tells the King that this is a wrong view, since the highest rule of dharma (*paramam dharmam*) is not to cause harm (*ahimsa*). To take life is not dharma, he declares; to abstain from taking life is dharma. Similarly, to steal is not dharma; not to steal is dharma. In this way Sudhanu enunciates the Ten Precepts. Indeed, he does more than that. Between the third and fourth precepts he inserts an extra precept, relating to the drinking of intoxicating liquor and spirits. It is interesting, though, that after enunciating the precepts he concludes by saying that the path of the *ten* right actions is dharma. Those who follow the path of the ten wrong actions, he tells the King, are reborn in hell. Those who follow the path of the ten right actions are reborn in heaven. In the present instance the path taken by the King is not the path to heaven; it is the path that leads to hell.

So impressed is King Sucandrima by this exposition of the Dharma that he releases all the living things he had brought together for the sacrifice, including the Kinnari, whereupon Sudhanu and Manohara, who have of course fallen in love, leave for the prince's own city – but this is only the beginning of the tale.[8]

Few of the Mahayana sutras survive in the original Sanskrit, most of them being extant only in Chinese and/or Tibetan translation. Among those still available in Sanskrit is the *Astasahasrikaprajnaparamita* or 'Perfection of Wisdom in 8,000 Lines', in which the Buddha, addressing the Arhant Subhuti, speaks of the signs of an irreversible Bodhisattva, that is, a Bodhisattva who, having renounced the possibility of nirvana for himself alone, is irreversible from Supreme Perfect Enlightenment for the benefit of all living beings. Such an irreversible Bodhisattva, the Buddha says, undertakes to observe the ten avenues or ways of wholesome action. He himself observes, and instigates others to observe, abstention from taking life and so on, down to abstention from wrong views:

It is quite certain that an irreversible Bodhisattva observes the ten ways of wholesome action, and instigates others to observe them, incites and encourages them to do so, establishes and confirms others in them. Even in his dreams he never commits offences against those ten precepts, and he does not nurse such offences in his mind. Even in his dreams an irreversible Bodhisattva keeps the ten wholesome paths of action present in his mind.[9]

One of the most important of the Mahayana sutras that do *not* survive in the original Sanskrit, but only in Chinese and Tibetan translation, is the *Vimalakirtinirdesa* or 'Exposition of Vimalakirti'. Here the purity of the *kusala-karma-pathas* or ten ways of skilful action, as the Ten Precepts are termed in this context, is said to be the *buddha-ksetra* or Buddha-field of the Bodhisattva.[10] It is from the ten paths of skilful action, moreover, that the Tathagata's body (*kaya*) is born.[11] The ten ways of skilful action are one of the ways in which, according to Vimalakirti, the Blessed Lord Sakyamuni expounds the Dharma here in the Saha world, and so on.[12] Finally, the Ten Precepts are mentioned in the celebrated third chapter of the

Suvarnaprabhasa Sutra or 'Sutra of Golden Light', the Chapter on Confession, which probably forms the original nucleus of the entire work,[13] and they are the principal subject-matter of the 'Discourse on the Ten Wholesome Ways of Action', a short work said to have been translated into Chinese from the Sanskrit.

Having shown that the Ten Precepts observed by members of the Western Buddhist Order actually were taught by the Buddha, and that references to them are found throughout the Tripitaka, we are now in a position to turn to the question of why the total transformation of the individual in which the act of Going for Refuge finds, and must find, expression, is represented more adequately by the Ten Precepts than by another set of precepts.

3

The Ten Precepts and Total Transformation

The human individual in his or her concrete reality is not simple but composite, consisting of various elements which can be distinguished even if not actually divided. These elements are variously enumerated. Pauline Christianity has its body, soul, and spirit; Upanisadic Hinduism its five *kosas* consisting, respectively, of food, breath, mind, intelligence, and bliss; Neoplatonism its soma, psyche, and pneuma, and so on.

In Buddhism the human individual is traditionally analysed into two, three, or five principal elements, each one of which is, of course, susceptible of further analysis. The twofold analysis resolves man into *nama* or 'name', by which is meant his subjective mental existence, and *rupa* or form, by which is meant his objective material existence. The threefold analysis resolves him into body (*kaya*), speech (*vak, vaca*), and mind (*citta*). In the more elaborate fivefold analysis the human individual is resolved into body (*rupa*), feeling (*vedana*), perception (*samjna*), volition (*samskara*), and consciousness (*vijnana*), collectively known as the five 'heaps' (*skandhas*).

Each set of elements, whether of a twofold, threefold, or fivefold nature, forms the centre of a vast and complex network of doctrinal, ethical, and symbolical correlations and associations which, in the course of centuries of development, grew more and more elaborate. What in the case of an ordinary unenlightened human being is simply name and form, in the case of a Buddha is *Dharmakaya* and *Rupakaya*, i.e. the 'body' in which he realizes the ultimate truth of things and the 'body' in which he continues to function in the world of appearances. Similarly, there is a correlation between the threefold composition of man, as consisting of body, speech, and mind, and the threefold composition of the Buddha, as consisting (according to the Yogacara systematization subsequently adopted by all the Mahayana schools) not only of a *Dharmakaya* and a *Rupakaya* (in this scheme termed the *Nirmanakaya* or 'created body') but also of a *Sambhogakaya* or 'body of glory' (literally 'body of mutual enjoyment') in which he functions on the higher spiritual planes and by means of which, in particular, he communicates with the Buddhas of other world-systems and with advanced Bodhisattvas.

In the case of the fivefold analysis of man, the five heaps are correlated with various other sets of five, both microcosmic and macrocosmic. There are the five Buddha families, the five knowledges (*jnana*), the five passions (*klesa*), the five elements, the five colours, and so on.

In addition, inasmuch as they are all analyses of the same 'object', i.e. the concrete reality of the human individual, the twofold, threefold, and fivefold analyses are naturally interrelated. 'Name' in the twofold analysis corresponds to speech and mind in the threefold analysis (and vice versa), while mind in the threefold analysis corresponds to feeling, perception, volition, and consciousness in the fivefold analysis (and vice versa). In other words, each analysis is an analysis of the total human being, and it is, of course, of the transformation of the total human being that we speak when we speak of the Ten Precepts and total transformation. Total transformation represents the complete transformation of the total individual in accordance with the highest imaginable ideal, the Ideal of Human Enlightenment.

But how is it that the *Ten* Precepts, in particular, should be associated with this process of total transformation, rather than the Five or the Eight, for instance? The answer to the question is implicit in what has already been said. The Precepts represent, in principle, the prolongation of the act of Going for Refuge into every aspect of one's existence. They represent, in other words, the total transformation of the individual who goes for Refuge, in accordance with the Ideal which that Going for Refuge implies.

The precepts which such an individual undertakes to observe, as the natural extension of his Going for Refuge, should therefore correspond to the principal elements of his existence. This means, in effect, that the division of the precepts should correspond to the 'division' of the individual human being as represented by one or another of the traditional Buddhist analyses.

The only set of precepts which fulfils this requirement is that of the Ten Precepts, which inasmuch as it comprises three precepts governing the body, four governing the speech, and three governing the mind, corresponds to the threefold analysis of man into body, speech, and mind. It is only the Ten Precepts, therefore, which bring out with sufficient clarity the fact that the Precepts represent the total transformation of the individual as the consequence of his Going for Refuge, and it is the Ten Precepts, therefore, that members of the Western Buddhist Order (Triratna Buddhist Order) undertake to observe.

Before we conclude our consideration of this topic, let me draw your attention to an interesting and significant fact. As we have seen, Buddhism analyses man into body, speech, and mind, and it is this triad that provides the framework for the Ten Precepts. References to 'body, speech, and mind' are, in fact, found throughout the Tripitaka, and it would appear that the triad goes back to the earliest period of Buddhism and formed part of the Buddha's own 'language'. As we know, that language was adopted, and in part adapted, from the existing Indian religious tradition or traditions, some terms and concepts indeed being subjected to radical redefinition and reinterpretation. The triad of body, speech, and mind did not form part of this already existing 'language'. Indeed, according to sources which I have not, as yet, had the opportunity of checking, the concept of man as consisting of body, speech, and mind is not to be found in the Vedas. If the Buddha did not think of it himself, and it seems unlikely that he did, then where did he get it from? He could only have got it – and this is the interesting and possibly significant fact to which I wanted to draw your attention – from the Zoroastrian tradition, in which the same triad occupies an extremely important place and where, as in Buddhism, there is a strong emphasis on a corresponding threefold purification.

This raises all sorts of fascinating questions concerning the relations between India and the Persian Empire, and between India and Central Asia, as well as concerning the extent to which Zoroastrianism may have influenced Buddhism, and Buddhism, in its turn, may have influenced Sufism. Fascinating as they are, however, these are questions which must be pursued on some future occasion. Meanwhile, we must proceed to our next topic.

4

The Ten Precepts as Principles of Ethics

First, a few definitions. By 'principle' is meant, in this connection, (a) 'a fundamental truth; a comprehensive law or doctrine, from which others are derived, or on which others are founded', and (b) 'a settled rule of action; a governing law of conduct; an opinion, attitude, or belief which exercises a directing influence on the life and behaviour; a rule (usually a right rule) of conduct consistently directing one's actions.' From this it is evident that the English word 'principle' (deriving ultimately from the Latin *principium, princeps*) has much in common with the Sanskrit word *dharma* (= Pali *dhamma*, Chinese *fa*, Tibetan *chos*). The Dharma taught by the Buddha, and to which as the second of the Three Jewels we go for Refuge, represents not only the fundamental truth or reality of things, as revealed in the Enlightened consciousness of the Buddha, but also that truth or reality as communicated to mankind in the form of a comprehensive law or doctrine from which there proceeds a governing law of conduct that exercises a directing influence on the life and behaviour of the individual 'dharmacari(ni)', i.e. the one who 'courses' (*carati*) in the Dharma-as-truth and the Dharma-as-righteousness. Thus the terms principle and dharma have a double significance, a significance that relates to both thought and action, theory and practice. Ethics is generally defined as 'the science of moral duty' or, more broadly, as 'the science of the ideal human character and the ideal ends of human action.' For the purpose of this discussion, it could be defined as that branch of knowledge which is concerned with human behaviour in so far as that behaviour is considered with regard to notions of right and wrong.

The expression 'the Ten Precepts' is, of course, English, and I have been using it as the equivalent of a number of different terms in Sanskrit and Pali. What we call the Ten Precepts is referred to, in the canonical sources, as the ten *silas* (a term which is applied, as we shall see later on, to more than one set of precepts), as the ten *siksapadas*, as the ten *kusala-karma-pathas*, and so on. (It must be emphasized that although the terms for them vary, the number of items comprised in the set remains unchanged, as does the actual content of each item.) Indeed, as we saw when referring to the fifty suttas of the *Anguttara-Nikaya* which are canonical sources of the Ten Precepts, what we call the Ten Precepts are in fact known by a wide variety of designations, their actual content however always remaining the same.

Perhaps the best-known term for the Ten Precepts is that which speaks of them as consisting of abstention from the ten *akusala-dharmas*, as they are called, and in the observance, practice, or cultivation of the ten *kusala-dharmas*.

'*Kusala*' is a very important term. In its broader significance it means clever, skilful, or expert in the sense of knowing how to act in a way that is beneficial rather than otherwise. *Kusala-karma* or skilful action thus is action which is directed towards securing, both for oneself and for others, the best possible results in terms of happiness, knowledge, and freedom, i.e. it is action which is constantly mindful of the law of *karma*, as well as of the painful, impermanent, and insubstantial nature of conditioned existence, and of the blissful, permanent, and 'empty' nature of the Unconditioned. *Kusala* thus is an ethical term, since it is a term which is applied, in the words of our definition of ethics, to 'human behaviour in so far as that behaviour is considered with regard to the notions of right and wrong.' Nor is that all. The term *kusala* is not applied to human behaviour considered with regard to notions of right or wrong in any merely abstract or 'comparative' sense. It is applied to it as considered with regard to a very definite and specific notion which the term *kusala* itself implies, and which it even embodies – i.e. the notion that 'right' is what conduces to the attainment of Enlightenment and 'wrong' what does not. The meaning of 'ethics' and the meaning of '*kusala*' therefore coincide. *Kusala* is not simply an ethical term. *Kusala* is itself the ethical.

But we can go further than that. The topic with which we are at present concerned is 'The Ten Precepts as Principles of Ethics'. We have seen that the best-known term for the Ten Precepts is the ten *kusala-dharmas*. We have also seen that the word 'principle' has much in common with the word 'dharma', even to the extent of their sharing the double connotation of relating to both thinking and doing, the theoretical and the practical, and that the word *kusala* coincides in meaning with 'ethical' and even with 'ethics'. Such being the case it should be clear, without further explanation, that what the Ten Precepts really represent are principles of ethics, or ethical principles. They are not rules, in the narrow, pettifogging sense of the term. They are not directly concerned with the minutiae of conduct, though they of course may be concerned with them indirectly.

The fact that, as we have seen, the observance of the Precepts represents the prolongation of the act of Going for Refuge into every aspect of one's existence, i.e. represents the total transformation of the individual who goes for Refuge in accordance with the Ideal which the Going for Refuge implies, means that one's behaviour comes to be increasingly governed by ten great ethical principles: the principles of non-violence or love, of non-appropriation or generosity, and so on. Thus the Ten Precepts are not rules, though rules may be founded on them, or derived from them. If we could think of the Precepts as being what in fact they are – ethical principles in accordance with which, as a result of our commitment to the Ideal of Enlightenment, we are doing our best to live – a good deal of confusion would be avoided. We would also find the Precepts themselves more inspiring.

Though the Precepts are most decidedly principles and not rules, yet rules in the sense of rules of training may, as I have said, be founded on them or derived from them. Moreover, both as principles and as rules the Precepts may be transmitted, within the appropriate ceremonial context, from teacher to disciple. To the topic of the Ten Precepts as Rules of Training we must now therefore turn.

5

The Ten Precepts as Rules of Training

The expression 'rules of training' is being used in this connection simply as the working equivalent of the Sanskrit *siksapadas* (Pali *sikkhapada*), otherwise rendered as 'moral commandments' or even as 'set of precepts'. In speaking of the Ten Precepts as rules of training we are, therefore, really speaking of the Ten Precepts as *siksapadas*, and for this reason it is necessary for us to inquire into the meaning of the term. *Pada* means 'step, footstep', and thus, in its applied meaning, 'case, lot, principle, part, constituent, characteristic, ingredient, item, thing, element'. In the present context it is best rendered as 'item', so that if *siksa* is 'training', *siksapada* is 'item of training'. *Siksa* is an interesting word, and one that forms part of a number of compounds. It derives from the desiderative of a verbal root meaning 'to be able', and therefore means 'learning, study, art, skill in', as well as 'teaching, training'. Thus it is approximately equivalent to the English word 'education', though since this derives from a Latin root meaning 'to draw out', whereas *siksa* derives from a Sanskrit root meaning 'to be able', there must be subtle differences in connotation between the two terms which educationists and *siksavadins* alike might find it useful to study. In speaking of the Ten Precepts as *siksapadas* we are, therefore, speaking of them as something to be learned, which means that we are speaking of them as *capable* of being learned. Indeed, in speaking of the Precepts as *siksapadas*, and therefore as capable of being learned (and one speaks of them in this way when 'taking' them from a teacher), one is at the same time speaking of oneself as one who is capable of learning them, i.e. capable of observing, or putting into practice, those ethical principles which, as we have already seen, are what the Ten Precepts primarily represent.

This emphasis on capability, learning, and training is, of course, very much in accordance with the spirit of Buddhism. Indeed, a well-known canonical formula declares the Buddha to be *purisadama-sarathi*, 'the Charioteer for the training of persons', and in more than one passage of the Tripitaka the Buddha himself describes the course of the spiritual life in terms of the gradual taming and training of a mettlesome young horse (cf. the Zen 'Ox-herding Pictures').

Now, learning implies its correlate, which is teaching; that one person learns implies that another teaches. In other words, just as education implies the existence of an educator, as well as the existence of one who is being educated, so a trainee implies the existence of a trainer, and the precepts the existence of a preceptor. The fact that the Ten Precepts, i.e. the ten great ethical principles, are *siksapadas* therefore means that the Ten Precepts are not only something to be learned (and, therefore, something one considers oneself capable of learning) but also something to be learned personally from a teacher. It is for this reason that the Ten Precepts are 'taken', at the time of 'ordination', from a teacher or preceptor, and the fact that in this context the Ten Precepts are termed *siksapadas* or things one is able and willing to learn means that they are taken not simply as ethical principles – ethical principles which henceforth will govern one's entire life – but also as principles which have to be learned, i.e. learned from a teacher.

Learning the Ten Precepts or ten great ethical principles in this way involves a number of things. It involves learning – in the sense of genuinely imbibing – the spirit as distinct from the letter of the Ten Precepts, learning how to apply the Ten Precepts to the affairs of everyday life, and learning how to confess breaches of the Ten Precepts and how to make any such breaches good. It also involves learning how to make and keep vows, in the sense of solemn promises to do something (e.g. to perform the Sevenfold Puja every day) or not to do something (e.g. not engage in sexual activity) for a certain specified period. Obviously there is a great deal that could be said on all these things, but time is short, there is still a good deal of ground to be covered, and we must pass on to the next topic.

6
The Ten Precepts as 'Mula-Pratimoksa'

The term *pratimoksa* (Pali *patimokkha*) is one of the most interesting and important terms in Early Buddhism or, more precisely, in what some scholars have called Early Monastic Buddhism. Despite the importance of the term, however, its real meaning, and even the nature of its original significance for the Buddhist community, are still matters of debate. With Childers, most modern scholars seem to regard it as being the same word as *pratimoksa* in the sense of 'binding, obligatory, obligation', so that *pratimoksa* (with a long *a*) means 'that which should be made binding'. A popular traditional explanation is that it means 'release from'– the release in question being the release (*moksa*) from (*prati*) a breach of the precepts obtained by a monk when he confesses his offence at the fortnightly meeting of the chapter of the monastic community. According to a Tibetan tradition, possibly deriving from Indian sources, *pratimoksa* is to be understood as 'individual liberation' (*so sor thar pa*) in the sense of the discipline that supports the individual liberation of the monk or nun.[14] Whatever the literal meaning of the term, and whatever the nature of its original significance for the Buddhist community may have been, there is no doubt that it very early came to be applied to the set of 150 rules binding on the individual monk – rules that formed the backbone, so to speak, of the code of between 227 and 263 rules (the traditions differ) governing the system of fully-developed coenobitical monasticism. By an extension of its meaning, the term also came to be applied, eventually, to the respective codes of all seven of the different socio-religious classes of persons comprising the Buddhist community. Besides the *bhikshu-pratimoksa* there was a *bhikshuni-pratimoksa* or code of rules for the nuns, a *pratimoksa* for the *siksamana* or female probationer, a *pratimoksa* for the *sramanera* or male novice, a *pratimoksa* for the *sramanerika* or female novice, a *pratimoksa* for the *upasaka* or male lay devotee, and a *pratimoksa* for the *upasika* or female lay devotee. Thus there were seven different *pratimoksas* or seven different sets of rules or sets of precepts which, though they were different as *pratimoksas*, were not always different in respect of the actual rules or precepts of which they consisted.

In those parts of the Buddhist world where the Precepts, i.e. the *pratimoksa*, took the place of the Going for Refuge as the highest common factor of Buddhism, the fact that the monks observed a much bigger number of precepts (the nuns, who were neither numerous nor influential, do not come into the picture), and the male and female lay devotees a very much smaller number, meant that the difference between the monks and the laity was exaggerated to such an extent that the unity of the Buddhist community was virtually disrupted. When we compare the different sets of precepts, however, from the 227–263 observed by the monk to the five (occasionally eight) observed by the lay devotee, we find that the precepts which they observe in common are of far greater importance than the precepts which are observed only by the monks. Indeed, we find that some of the precepts observed only by the monks represent, in fact, not *additional* precepts so much as either (a) a more thoroughgoing application of the precepts observed by the laity, i.e. the precepts which the monks and laity observe in common, or (b) an application of those precepts to certain more specific conditions, especially the conditions of coenobitical monastic life.

We also find that some of the precepts observed only by the monks are of no real ethical significance, being in some cases concerned with matters of a quite trivial nature and demonstrably the product of social conditions prevailing at the time of the Buddha or shortly after. Unfortunately, it is 'precepts' of this sort which, only too often, have been emphasized at the expense of that part of the *bhikshu* code of rules which is of a genuinely ethical character, i.e. at the expense of what I am calling the '*Mula-Pratimoksa*', with the result that the division between the monks and the laity has widened, in some Buddhist countries, to so great an extent that one is justified in speaking of there being, in the religious or spiritual sense, first-class Buddhists and second-class Buddhists.

If the spiritual unity of the Buddhist community is to be preserved from disruption, therefore, what is needed is (a) an uncompromising assertion of the primacy of the Going for Refuge as the fundamental Buddhist act, and (b) a drastic reduction of the rules comprising the seven different *pratimoksas* to those precepts of genuinely ethical significance which they have in common, together with a firm insistence on the necessity of one's actually observing those precepts. If the different *pratimoksas* are 'reduced' in this way, what one will have left will be, in effect, the Ten Precepts – though inasmuch as they include three purely 'mental' precepts the Ten Precepts are, in fact, more comprehensive in scope than are all the seven *pratimoksas* combined.

The Ten Precepts therefore constitute the '*Mula-Pratimoksa*' or 'Fundamental *Pratimoksa*', as I have called it, the term being not a traditional one – though it might well have been – but one of my own devising. It is the Ten Precepts in the sense of the ten great ethical principles which, in reality, all practising Buddhists – and there is really no other kind – have in common. When one has refined the crude ore of popular Buddhist ethical and pseudo-ethical observance, whether 'monastic' or 'lay', when one has removed the accretions and excrescences, and picked out the foreign bodies, one finds that one then has left the scintillating diamond, the gleaming gold, and the pure crystal, and so on, of the Ten Precepts – that is, one has left those ten great ethical principles which, as prolongations of the act of Going for Refuge into every aspect of one's existence, govern and eventually transform one's life.

It is for this reason that the Ten Precepts have been adopted by the Western Buddhist Order in preference to any of the other traditional sets of precepts, whether they are merely mentioned in the Buddhist scriptures or actually transmitted by the various Buddhist schools. For the Western Buddhist Order the Ten Precepts, as '*Mula-Pratimoksa*', are in fact the discipline that supports the 'individual liberation' not only of the monk and the nun, but of all members of the Buddhist community irrespective of lifestyle.

Since there is only one set of precepts, i.e. the Ten Precepts, so far as the Western Buddhist Order is concerned there is only one 'ordination', i.e. the Dharmacari(ni) ordination, which means that in the Western Buddhist Order one is not ordained as a monk, or as a nun, or as a female probationer, or as a male novice, or as a female novice, or as a male lay devotee, or as a female lay devotee, but simply and solely as a full, practising member of the Sangha or Buddhist Spiritual

Community, though it is of course open to one to observe, as personal vows, any of the rules traditionally observed by the monk, or the nun, and so on. Strictly speaking, these rules are not observed *in addition* to the Ten Precepts but as representing the more intensive practice of one or more of the Precepts within a certain specific situation or for a certain purpose.

Not being a *bhikshu*, a member of the Western Buddhist Order does not wear the stitched yellow garment of the *bhikshu*, and not being an *upasaka* he does not wear the white garments of the *upasaka*. He wears the ordinary 'lay' dress of the society to which he belongs, though without the implication that because he is not a monk he must therefore be a layman in the traditional Buddhist sense.

Thus from the reduction of the rules comprising the seven different *pratimoksas* to the Ten Precepts or '*Mula-Pratimoksa*' there follows a reduction – or rather an elevation – of the various socio-religious groups within the Buddhist community to one great Spiritual Community or Mahasangha. Such a reduction represents a return to, and a renewed emphasis upon, the basics of Buddhism. It can be regarded as innovative only by adopting a standpoint from which those basics are ignored or from which they cannot be seen for the accretions and excrescences by which they have become overlaid.

As we saw when considering the sources of the Ten Precepts in the *Majjhima-Nikaya*, Sariputta and the

Buddha are represented in the *Sevitabba-asevitabba-sutta* as in turn expounding the Ten Precepts in front of an assembly of *bhikshus* or monks, though we may be sure that they were not 'monks' in the full coenobitical sense of later times. Among the fifty suttas of the *Anguttara-Nikaya*, another canonical source of the Ten Precepts, there are three suttas in which the Ten Precepts are referred to as being observed (or not observed) by womenfolk (*matugamo*), by a female lay devotee, and by a female lay devotee who dwells at home with (or without) confidence, respectively.[15] The Ten Precepts are thus shown to have been the common observance of persons of different socio-religious classes. Moreover, the *Sevitabba-asevitabba-sutta* concludes with the Buddha saying, with regard to all the teachings given in the sutta, including that of the Ten Precepts:

> And, Sariputta, if all nobles ... all brahmans ... all merchants ... all workers could thus understand the meaning in full of this that was spoken by me in brief, for a long time it would be for their welfare and happiness. And, Sariputta, if the world with the devas, with the Maras and Brahmas, and if the generations of recluses and brahmans, devas and men could thus understand the meaning in full of this that was spoken of by me in brief, for a long time it would be for their welfare and happiness.[16]

This would suggest that the Ten Precepts represent the norm of ethical behaviour not only for all Buddhists but for all human beings – indeed, for all forms of self-conscious sentient existence.

Such being the case it is the Ten Precepts which, together with the Three Jewels or Three Refuges, constitute the surest possible basis for unity among Buddhists. The time has come for Buddhists to give greater emphasis to what is common and fundamental rather than to what is distinctive and superficial, and in this respect the Western Buddhist Order has, perhaps, given a lead to the rest of the Buddhist world. In the Ten Precepts we have a set of ethical principles that is both clear and comprehensive. There is no point whatever in taking a large number of precepts in the knowledge that one will not, in fact, be observing some of them. Such a proceeding, unfortunately so common in many parts of the Buddhist world, is extremely demoralizing in its effects, and in fact undermines the whole basis of the ethical and spiritual life. In the Western Buddhist Order, therefore, the Ten Precepts are not only seen as '*Mula-Pratimoksa*', but also taken with the intention that they should be observed. Indeed, they are taken with the intention that they should be observed more and more perfectly, as an expression of an ever-deepening commitment to the Three Jewels.

7

The Ten Precepts and Other Ethical Formulae

The Ten Precepts have already been spoken of as *kusala-dharmas*, which as we have seen really means ethical principles, as *siksapadas* or rules of training, and as avenues or ways of skilful (or wholesome) action, as well as in terms of their being the '*Mula-Pratimoksa*' implicitly for all Buddhists and explicitly for the members of the Western Buddhist Order. It now remains for us to relate the Ten Precepts to certain of the other ethical formulae which are found figuring so prominently in Buddhist literature and Buddhist life.

One of the most important of these is, of course, the formula of the Noble Eightfold Path, to which the Ten Precepts can be related through the formula of the three *skandhas* or 'groups' or, for that matter, through one or the other of the two broadly equivalent formulae of the three *sampadas* or 'attainments' and the three *siksas* or 'trainings', as well as through the formula of the three ways of skilful action. The three groups are the noble group of *sila* or ethics, *samadhi* or concentration and meditation, and *prajna* or wisdom. Since the first seven precepts are concerned with bodily and vocal conduct they comprise the noble group of *sila* or ethics, and since in terms of the Noble Eightfold Path ethics consists of Right (or Perfect) Speech, Action, and Livelihood, it is clear that the first seven precepts correspond to the third, fourth, and fifth stages of the Noble Eightfold Path. Similarly, since the eighth and ninth precepts are concerned with that part of mental conduct which comprises the noble group of *samadhi* or concentration and meditation, and since in terms of the Noble Eightfold Path concentration and meditation consists of Right (or Perfect) Effort, Mindfulness, and Concentration, the eighth and ninth precepts must correspond to the sixth, seventh, and eighth steps of the Noble Eightfold Path. Finally, since the tenth precept is concerned with that part of mental conduct which comprises the noble group of wisdom, and since in terms of the Noble Eightfold Path wisdom consists of Right (or Perfect) Emotion and Understanding (or Vision), the tenth precept must correspond to the first and second steps of the Noble Eightfold Path. All this could, no doubt, be made clearer with the help of a diagram.

In any case, it will be noticed that although I have spoken of all ten precepts as ethical principles, in the present connection it is only the first seven precepts that are said to comprise the noble group of *sila* or ethics. The contradiction is more apparent than real. The term ethics can be used in two senses, a broader and a narrower. Ethics in the broad sense is the art or science of human conduct and character as possessing value in relation to a standard or ideal, and it is in this sense of the term that the Ten Precepts are ethical principles. As such, ethics is more or less identical with religion in its more practical aspect. Ethics in the narrow sense is concerned with external, bodily and vocal behaviour, and it is in this sense of the term that the first seven precepts are said to comprise the noble group of ethics.

Besides relating the Ten Precepts to certain other ethical formulae, it is also necessary to distinguish it from another formula similarly termed. This is the formula of the Ten Precepts observed by the *sramanera* or novice monk, a set of rules which comprises, in addition to the Five Precepts ('abstention from sexual misconduct' being in this context replaced by 'abstention from non-celibacy'), the precepts of abstaining from untimely meals, from song, dance, music, and indecent shows, from the use of flower-garlands, scents, unguents, and ornaments, from the use of luxurious beds and seats, and from handling gold and silver. It will be readily seen that these precepts are of a very different character from the precepts making up the second half of the '*Mula-Pratimoksa*' since, however useful and even necessary they may

be to certain people or in certain circumstances, they
are hardly of fundamental importance.

8
The Ten Precepts and Lifestyle

Most Order members will be familiar with the aphorism 'Commitment is primary, life-style secondary.' What its original source was, and how it came to be introduced into the FWBO, is a matter of some uncertainty. I may even have introduced it myself, in which case I have quite a lot to answer for, since from the day of its introduction the aphorism seems to have been the innocent cause of a good deal of confusion and misunderstanding. In the first place it has sometimes been assumed that 'secondary' meant 'unimportant', or even 'irrelevant', with the result that the aphorism was understood to mean that, provided you were committed, i.e. committed to the Three Jewels, it was a matter of indifference what lifestyle you followed and that, indeed, no lifestyle was intrinsically better – or worse – than any other, and that to try to make it out to be so was a sign of intolerance. However, 'secondary' most certainly does not mean 'unimportant', and when it is said that commitment is primary and lifestyle secondary what this means is that the lifestyle of a Buddhist – i.e. of one committed to the Three Jewels – is dependent on, or follows from, or is an expression of, the fact that he is thus committed or, in more traditional language, that he goes for Refuge.

Reference to the dictionary definition of 'lifestyle' will help to make this clearer. According to *Collins English Dictionary* (1979), lifestyle is 'the particular attitudes, beliefs, habits, or behaviour associated with an individual or group.' Since things like attitudes, beliefs, habits, and behaviour can be either skilful or unskilful it follows that the lifestyle which they collectively represent can be either skilful or unskilful too. Not all lifestyles, therefore, can be expressions of one's commitment to the Three Jewels. Similarly with the Ten Precepts and lifestyle: just as the Ten Precepts themselves are an expression of one's Going for Refuge, so one's lifestyle is an expression of one's observance of the Ten Precepts. One could therefore say that the Ten Precepts are primary and lifestyle secondary, though perhaps it would be better for the sake of consistency to say that commitment is primary, the observance of the Ten Precepts secondary, and lifestyle tertiary, by which one would mean that although all three are of importance, the second is important as an expression of the first, and the third important as an expression of the second. 'Lifestyle' does not, therefore, represent some ethically neutral way of life which can be combined, without modification, with the pursuit of Enlightenment. For this reason one's lifestyle is something that is open to criticism, so that one cannot, as a Buddhist, rebut criticism of such things as one's particular attitudes, beliefs, habits, or behaviour with the indignant rejoinder, 'Oh, but that's my lifestyle', as though this at once placed the matter not only beyond criticism but beyond discussion.

One of the main sources of the confusion and misunderstanding to which I referred is, no doubt, the word 'style'. In the context of the visual arts one can speak of the baroque style and the rococo style without necessarily implying that one is better than the other. Similarly, in the context of literary criticism one can speak of a plain style and an artificial style, and in the context of book production of the distinctive house styles of different publishers, without thereby implying the absolute superiority of one style over another. But one can speak of lifestyles in this way only to a very limited extent. In other words, very few lifestyles are truly neutral in character. One can, indeed, speak of a rural lifestyle and an urban lifestyle without necessarily implying an ethical judgement, but one can hardly speak of the lifestyle of a slaughterman or of a prostitute – to take two quite extreme examples – without, as a Buddhist, thereby implying a very definite ethical judgement indeed.

With this brief discussion of the Ten Precepts and lifestyle – a topic of perhaps more limited interest than the seven topics preceding it – we conclude our discussion of the Ten Precepts collectively and, therewith, the first part of this paper. The discussion of the eight topics into which the whole discussion of the Ten Precepts was broken down has, I hope, helped us to achieve a more comprehensive view of the Ten Pillars of Buddhism in their collective majesty. In the second part of the paper we shall be dealing with each of the Ten Precepts separately. This will enable us, I trust, to see each pillar in its individual splendour. As before, I shall try to avoid losing myself in details, and instead concentrate on the spiritual significance of the great principles involved, and on some of their more practical consequences. I shall, also, seek to enhance our appreciation of the splendour and beauty of the Ten Precepts, not only by speaking of one pillar as a pillar of diamond, one as a pillar of gold, one as a pillar of crystal, and so on, but also by explaining why a particular pillar is associated with a particular precious stone or precious metal.

Part Two

The Ten Precepts Individually

The First Precept
The Principle of Abstention from Killing Living Beings; or Love

The more important an ethical principle is, the more likely it is that it will be so obvious as to be overlooked or neglected. This is certainly true of the principle with which we are at present concerned. *Of course* one should not kill human beings, or even animals (though important exceptions are often made when the human being happens to be of a different race, religion, or nationality, or when the animal is wanted for food or sport, or when it is more valuable dead than alive)! *Of course* murder is wrong! Murder is a crime, a sin! But this acknowledgement once made, most people assume that since they have never personally killed a living being, and are unlikely to do so in the future, the matter does not really concern them and they can get on with their lives without giving it a further thought. Even Buddhists tend to think that because they are observing the First Precept anyway there is no need for them to think about it. After all, there are much more interesting and important aspects of the Dharma for one to concern oneself with, and simple and obvious things

65

like the First Precept can be safely left to the dull and unintelligent while one explores the secrets of Tantra or the mysteries of Zen.

But the truth is that the First Precept is not to be disposed of in this way. The principle of abstention from killing living beings, or love, in fact runs very deep in life, both social and spiritual, and its ramifications are not only very extensive but enormously significant. Within the specifically Buddhist context of the Ten Precepts it is the most direct and most important manifestation of the spiritual and existential act of Going for Refuge. Moreover, it is a principle that finds expression, in one way or another, and to a greater or lesser degree, not only in the First Precept itself, but in all the other Precepts as well. For this reason it merits our serious consideration.

Let us begin by considering the precise significance of 'Abstention from Killing Living Beings' or, in terms of the positive formulation of the Precepts, the precise significance of 'Love'. (If each Precept is a pillar of diamond, or gold, or crystal, and so on, its negative and positive formulations are the dark and bright sides of the pillar as it stands fronting the sun.) Though the literal meaning of *atipata* is 'striking down', the word *panatipata* – for the sake of convenience I shall use the simpler and more familiar Pali forms – actually means destruction of life, slaying, killing, murder. But why should killing be wrong? One explanation, of course, is that as the expression of a mental state rooted in greed, hatred, and delusion (or at least two of these), killing is an unskilful act in the sense that it brings suffering upon the doer and prevents him from attaining Enlightenment. But we can go deeper than that. Generally speaking, to kill a living being means to inflict upon him the greatest of all sufferings or evils, for inasmuch as life itself is the greatest good, so the greatest suffering, or greatest evil, that can befall one is to be deprived of life.

Now one cannot do to a man what he regards as evil except against his will, that is to say, one cannot do it except by force or violence (*himsa*), by which is meant not only physical force but also such things as emotional blackmail and fraud. Violence indeed consists in our doing to another person, by whatever means, what he does not want us to do to him. Since what he least wants us to do to him is to deprive him of life, which being the greatest good is what he most values, to kill him is to commit the greatest violence against him that it is possible to commit. We ourselves, of course, do not want to be deprived of life, any more than he does, so that to kill him is not only the extreme of violence; it is also, at the same time, the absolute negation of the solidarity of one living being *qua* living being with another and, in the case of human beings, of the solidarity of one human being *qua* human being with another.

Non-violence (*ahimsa*) is said to be the highest rule of religion (*paramam dharmam*), because violence (*himsa*) is the basest rule of irreligion and – barring certain refinements introduced by the perverted imagination of certain monsters of iniquity – the most extreme form that unethical behaviour can take. Violence and killing are, in fact, closely connected, killing being the most extreme form of violence and, in a sense, its logical consequence. The First Precept is, therefore, often spoken of in terms of abstention from violence, though since killing in any case presupposes violence, and since (as we have seen) the Pali word *panatipata* means destruction of life, the precept is probably best spoken of as abstention from killing.

Be that as it may, the deeper significance of the First Precept consists in the fact that killing is wrong because it represents the extremest form that the negation of one ego by another, or the assertion of one ego at the expense of another, can possibly take – though, paradoxically, the negation of another's ego is, at the same time, in principle the negation of one's own. Killing is tantamount to a complete rejection of the Golden Rule, and without the Golden Rule there can be no human society, no culture, and no spiritual life. In its Buddhist form the Golden Rule finds expression in two well-known verses of the *Dhammapada*:

All (living beings) are terrified of punishment (*danda*); all fear death. Making comparison (of others) with oneself, one should neither kill nor cause to kill.

All (living beings) are terrified of punishment (*danda*); to all, life is dear. Making comparison (of others) with oneself, one should neither kill nor cause to kill.[17]

Here the Golden Rule is stated in negative terms: you should *not* do unto others what you would *not* that others should do unto you. It can also be stated positively: you should *do* unto others as you would they should *do* unto you. (George Bernard Shaw does, of course, say 'Do not do unto others as you would they should do unto you. They may not have the same tastes', but this is only to draw attention to the fact that it is the spirit of the Golden Rule that matters, not the letter.) Just as abstention from killing represents the Golden Rule in its negative form, so the cultivation of Love represents the Golden Rule in its positive form. As Shelley so finely says:

The great secret of morals is love; or a going out of our own nature, and an identification of ourselves with the beautiful which exists in thought, action, or person, not our own. A man, to be greatly good, must imagine intensely and comprehensively; he must put himself in the place of another and of many others; the pains and pleasures of his species must become his own.

This putting oneself in the place of another amounts to the same thing as the 'making comparison (of others) with oneself' of which the *Dhammapada* speaks. In the *Bodhicaryavatara* or 'Entry into the Way of Enlightenment' Santideva gives to this same principle what is probably its sublimest expression in Buddhist literature. After describing how, by pondering upon the excellencies of solitude, a man stills vain imaginations and strengthens his Thought of (or Will to) Enlightenment (*Bodhicitta*), he proceeds:

First he will diligently foster the thought that his fellow creatures are the same as himself. 'All have the same sorrows, the same joys as I, and I must guard them like myself. The body, manifold of parts in its divisions of members, must be preserved as a whole; and so likewise this manifold universe has its sorrow and its joy in common. Although my pain may bring no hurt to other bodies, nevertheless it is a pain to me, which I cannot bear because of the love of self; and though I cannot in myself feel the pain of another, it is a pain to him which he cannot bear because of the love of self. I must destroy the pain of another as though it were my own, because it is a pain; I must show kindness to others, for they are creatures as I am myself.... Then, as I would guard myself from evil repute, so I will frame a spirit of helpfulness and tenderness towards others.'

By constant use the idea of an 'I' attaches itself to foreign drops of seed and blood, although the thing exists not. Then why should I not conceive my fellow's body as my own self? That my body is foreign to me is not hard to see. I will think of myself as a sinner, of others as oceans of virtue; I will cease to live as self, and will take as myself my fellow-creatures. We love our hands and other limbs, as members of the body; then why not love other living beings, as members of the universe? By constant use man comes to imagine that his body, which has no self-being, is a 'self'; why then should he not conceive his 'self' to lie in his fellows also? Thus in doing service to others pride, admiration, and desire of reward find no place, for thereby we satisfy the wants of our own self. Then, as thou wouldst guard thyself against suffering and sorrow, so exercise the spirit of helpfulness and tenderness towards the world.[18]

This is what is known as the practice of equality of self and others (*paratmasamata*) and substitution of self and others (*paratmaparivartana*). Blake gives succinct expression to much the same principle when he declares: 'The most sublime act is to put another before you.' Whether described in terms of making comparison of others with oneself, however, or in terms of the substitution of self and others, or in any other way, the Love which is the positive form of the First Precept is no mere flabby sentiment but the vigorous expression of an imaginative identification with other living beings. 'Love' is in fact far too weak a word for the positive counterpart of non-killing or non-violence, and even *maitri* (Pali *metta*) is not altogether satisfactory. Just as killing represents the absolute negation of another person's being, 'Love', as we must perforce call it, represents its absolute affirmation. As such it is not erotic love, or parental love, or even friendly love. If it is love at all, it is a cherishing, protecting, maturing love which has the same kind of effect on the spiritual being of others as the light and heat of the sun have on their physical being.

Such 'Love' is, of course, quite rare. Violence is much more common, even though it only exceptionally takes the form of actual killing. Putting things in another way, it may be said that human beings operate much more frequently in accordance with the power mode than in accordance with the love mode. But what is power? In this context power means simply the capacity to use force, violence being the actual use of that capacity to negate the being of another person, whether wholly or in part. To operate in accordance with the power mode means, therefore, to relate to other living beings in terms of violence, or in such a way as to negate rather than affirm their being. To operate in accordance with the love mode is the opposite of this. Since every living being, including every human being, has the capacity to use force, to however limited an extent, every living being possesses power, in however limited a degree. Human beings possess more power, both material and mental, than any other living beings, both in relation to their own species and in relation to other species.

From this point of view observance of the First Precept means that, as a result of our imaginative identification with others, we not only abstain from actually killing living beings but operate more and more in accordance with the love mode and less and less in accordance with the power mode. In this way there takes place within us a change so great as to amount to a change in our centre of gravity, so to speak, and this change manifests both as observance of the First Precept and, to the extent that their individual natures permit, as observance of all the other Precepts as well.

It will not, of course, be possible for even the most faithful observer of the First Precept to operate all at once in terms of the love mode, eschewing the power mode completely. We live in a world dominated by the power mode. The love mode comes into operation only in the case of exceptional individuals, and even they may not always find it possible, or even desirable, to act in accordance with the love mode. In this connection two principles may be laid down. (a) Whenever one has to operate in accordance with the power mode, the power mode must always be subordinated to the love mode. A simple, everyday example of such subordination is when the parent, out of love for the child, forcibly restrains him from doing something that will harm him. (b) Within the Spiritual Community it is impossible to act in accordance with the power mode, for by its very nature as a voluntary association of free individuals sharing certain common goals the Spiritual Community is based on the love mode. This means that, should an Order member so far forget himself as to relate to another Order member in terms of force or violence, he to that extent places himself outside the Spiritual Community and ceases, in fact, to be an Order member. Acts of violence between Order members are, therefore, the most serious breach of the unity and solidarity of the Order that can possibly be imagined, even as the best conceivable means of strengthening that unity and solidarity are thoughts, words, and deeds of love.

Besides operating in accordance with the power mode only to the extent that the power mode is subordinated to the love mode, Order members should do their best to switch from the power mode to the love mode in as many different ways as possible, and to extend the Principle of Abstention from Killing Living Beings, or Principle of Love, into as many different areas of life as possible, both individual and collective. Observance of the First Precept will, in fact, naturally result in one's being a vegetarian, in one's refusing to have oneself, or to assist or encourage others in having, an abortion, in one's feeling concern for the environment, and in one's being opposed not only to the production and deployment of nuclear weapons but to the manufacture of all armaments whatsoever, as well as in many other things.

Not that the observance of the First Precept consists simply in one's doing, or not doing, a certain stated number of things of this sort. Non-violence, or Love, is a principle, and being a principle there is no limit to the number of ways in which it can be applied. No one is so unskilful in his conduct that his practice of non-violence, or Love, could not be worse, and no one is so skilful in his conduct that his practice of it could not be better. As the most direct manifestation of one's Going for Refuge, the potentialities of non-violence, or Love, are infinite.

In terms of the precious stone of which it consists, the First Precept is a pillar of diamond. It is a pillar of diamond because the diamond is the most valuable of all precious stones, and capable of being cut into facets so as to make a brilliant. It is also the hardest substance known, even as the love mode is 'stronger' than the power mode and capable of 'overcoming' it in all its forms.

The Second Precept
The Principle of Abstention from Taking the Not-Given; or Generosity

Just as the First Precept is not simply a matter of not killing, even though the negative form of the Precept is couched in those terms, so the Second Precept is not simply a matter of not stealing; and in this case the negative form of the Precept does in fact make this quite clear. *Adinnadana veramani* means, literally, abstention (*veramani*) from seizing or grasping (*adana*) that which is not given (*adinna*). In other words it means not taking or appropriating that which another is not willing to give.

Since violence consists in our doing to another what he does not want us to do to him, taking the not-given is therefore a form of violence. It is a violence committed not in respect of the actual person of the other, as in the case of physical attack, but in respect of his property; though it is arguable that violence in respect of property is indirectly violence in respect of the person inasmuch as property by very definition belongs to someone, in this case the other, and is *his* property. (This of course raises the whole question of ownership, about which I shall have something to say in a minute.)

Since taking the not-given is a form of violence, all that has been said about force and violence in connection with the First Precept – including what has been said about the Golden Rule, and about the power mode and the love mode – can be taken as also said about the Second Precept, and applied accordingly. For this reason it will not be necessary for us to deal with the Second Precept at quite the same length as the First. After dealing with Generosity, the positive form of the Second Precept, I shall make a few remarks on three points arising in connection with its observance, and then conclude by dealing, very briefly, with the subject of ownership.

In 'Song of Myself', one of the earliest sections of *Leaves of Grass* to be composed, Walt Whitman announces:

> *Behold, I do not give lectures or a little charity,*
> *When I give I give myself.*

These lines illustrate the difference between Love, in the sense that the term was used in connection with the First Precept, and Generosity, in the sense that the word was used in connection with the Second. Love gives itself – that is to say, Love is a self-giving of person to person or, if you like, a surrender of person to person ('surrender' here meaning the complete abandonment of any advantage derived from the power mode). Generosity is a giving of property to person, and is an expression of Love. Indeed, where Love exists in its fullness there is no question even of Generosity, because Love is, in the last resort, incompatible with the sense of ownership and, therefore, with property, and thinks not so much in terms of Generosity as in terms of common 'ownership' or Sharing.

Shakespeare gives matchless expression to the paradoxical implications of this mutual 'Generosity' in one of his poems. (When I started preparing this paper I did not know that I would be quoting the poets so much, or that the poets would have so much to say on the subject of ethics.) Speaking of the mutual love of the Phoenix and the Turtle, he assures us:

> *So between them love did shine,*
> *That the turtle saw his right*
> *Flaming in the phoenix' sight;*
> *Either was the other's mine.*

> *Property was thus appalled,*
> *That the self was not the same;*
> *Single nature's double name*
> *Neither two nor one was called.*

Reason, in itself confounded,
Saw division grow together;
To themselves yet either neither,
Simple were so well compounded,

That it cried, 'How true a twain
Seemeth this concordant one!
Love hath reason, reason none,
If what parts can so remain.'

For Buddhism it is not so much a question of a twain seeming 'a concordant one' as of the whole Spiritual Community being such. Ultimately, as in the case of the Bodhisattva, Generosity reaches a point where the giver, the gift, and the recipient of the gift, cease to be distinguishable. It is this kind of Generosity that constitutes the positive form of the Second Precept, as well as the true counterpart, within the context of so-called property relations, of the positive form of the First Precept, i.e. Love.

The three points that arise in connection with the observance of the Second Precept concern ways of taking the not-given not specifically mentioned in the Buddhist tradition, gratitude, and indebtedness.

Since the Second Precept is, like all the other Precepts, primarily an ethical principle, it follows that we should not be content to confine ourselves to such applications of this principle as are specifically mentioned in the Buddhist scriptures. To confine ourselves in this way is to be guilty of ethical formalism, and ethical or pseudoethical formalism is one of the greatest enemies of Buddhism and of the spiritual life generally.

Among the various forms of taking the not-given which are not, to the best of my knowledge, known to Buddhist tradition (at least in the sense that abstention from them is not explicitly enjoined in connection with the Second Precept) are taking the time or taking the energy of another person against his or her wishes. We take time from another person when we force ourselves upon them when they have work to do, or when we force them to listen to talk which they have no wish to hear. This form of *adinnadana* or seizing or grasping the not-given is very common in modern social life (and not entirely unknown in ancient social life either, if we can believe Horace). Buddhists should do their best to avoid it, both inside and outside the Spiritual Community.

Taking the energy or vitality of another person against his or her wishes, which is closely connected with taking their time, is even more pernicious. Here one forces oneself upon another to such an extent, and compels them to listen to one's complaints, or appeals or tirades, for so long, that one eventually reduces them to a state of physical prostration, emotional exhaustion, and even nervous collapse.

Having drained another of their energy in this way, one may sometimes be heard to remark, either to one's victim or to some third party, 'I really enjoyed our little chat.' Human vampires of this sort are sometimes quite oblivious to the damage they do and fail to realize, if they are Buddhists, that they are breaking the Second Precept – and probably the First as well.

This is not to say that one may not take the time and energy of another, and even drain them, if one really needs to do so and if they are themselves willing to give their time and energy to this extent – which brings us to the subject of gratitude.

When you are given something you need, and especially when you are given it freely and willingly, the natural human response is to feel grateful. If you do not feel grateful something is wrong. Either the need itself is an unhealthy and even neurotic need, and hence not really capable of satisfaction (and one can hardly feel gratitude for a satisfaction that has not been experienced), or else your attitude is one of seizing and grasping regardless of whether the other person wants to give you what you need or not. Real gratitude can be felt only when you take from another both what you genuinely need and what they are willing to give. Gratitude can be felt, therefore, only by the mature and integrated, i.e. by true individuals, and true individuals not only feel but express gratitude.

It is perhaps significant that within the Western Buddhist Order and the Friends of the Western Buddhist Order expressions of gratitude have become increasingly common in recent years. This is a very positive development indeed. Formerly one hardly heard an expression of gratitude from one year's end to the other. Now, I am glad to say, expressions of gratitude are to be heard if not every day then at least two or three times a week.

The connection between indebtedness and the Second Precept is not always appreciated. Wilfully to withhold from another the money, for example, that one owes him – money which he wishes one to repay, and of which he may be in need – is to be guilty of taking that which is not given and, therefore, of violence. It also means that so long as a debt is undischarged one cannot, in fact, give *dana*, i.e. cannot practise Generosity, for one's so-called *dana* will be no more than a robbing of Peter to give to Paul – and Paul himself, if he knows what the situation is, will be virtually a receiver of stolen goods. Indebtedness in this context does not, of course, include being in debt to a bank for a loan which must be repaid by a certain date, and on which one is in the meantime paying interest. But it certainly does include being in debt to friends and relations, whether in respect of money, goods, or services, as well as being in debt to tradesmen, professional advisers, and the state.

This is the reason why prospective Order members are asked, before ordination, to discharge all debts, since otherwise their observance of one, at least, of the Precepts taken at the time of ordination will be seriously vitiated from the very outset.

Within the Order itself, that is to say, between Order members themselves, whether individually or 'collectively', there can be no question of taking that which is not given, and therefore no question of indebtedness in the ordinary sense, since although members of the Order do not hold their property in common it is widely accepted that, within the Spiritual Community, common ownership is the ideal. In any case, by virtue of their observance of the Second Precept, all members of the Order are deeply imbued with the principle of Generosity, or Sharing, and do their best to practise it in their relations with one another.

This brings us to the question of ownership in general. According to Proudhon, 'property is theft', but this does not help us very much. If property is theft there is no one who is not a thief, since there is no one of legal age who does not own property, and the question of ownership – whether common or otherwise – can hardly be decided by a community of thieves. We shall therefore have to start all over again. There is no doubt that property is inequitably distributed, in the sense of not being distributed in accordance with the genuine needs of people, but what can we do about it?

For a Buddhist the answer is to be found in the combined operation of the power mode and the love mode, the power mode of course operating in subordination to the love mode. In a democratic country, a more equitable distribution of property or wealth can be achieved through legislation, which means in effect the forcible expropriation of the minority by the majority, as well as by the encouragement of a deeper understanding and a more effective practice, on the grandest possible scale, of the principle of Generosity, or Sharing. The latter, as I need hardly remind you, is particularly the responsibility of a body like the Western Buddhist Order. More than that it is not possible for me to say on this occasion. The subject of ownership is a vast one, but we shall surely not go far wrong if we adhere, and encourage others to adhere, to the principle of Generosity, or Sharing.

Since gold is the most precious of all metals, and a common medium of commercial exchange, the Second Precept is a pillar of gold. 'Yellow, glistering gold', as Shakespeare calls it, is the most malleable and ductile of all metals, and therefore well represents the infinite adaptability to the needs of living beings which Generosity, the positive form of the Second Precept, represents. Gold is quite unalterable by heat, moisture, and most corrosive agents. In the same way, Generosity is not affected by the conditions under which it has to function, or by such things as ingratitude in the recipient.

The Third Precept
The Principle of Abstention from Sexual Misconduct; or Contentment

It will help us to understand the Third Precept, especially in its positive form as Contentment, if we can see it within the context of traditional Buddhist cosmology. That cosmology reveals to us what may be described as a three-tiered universe. Mundane existence is divided into three horizontal layers, as it were, the second of which is higher than the first, in the sense of being more refined, positive, blissful, and luminous, and the third higher than the second. These three 'layers' are the planes, worlds, or spheres – the terminology varies – of sensuous desire (*kama*), of archetypal form (*rupa*), and of no archetypal form (*arupa*). The plane of sensuous desire comprises (in ascending order) the hell world, the world of hungry ghosts, the world of *asuras* or anti-gods, the animal world, the human world, and the world of the (lower) gods, from the four great kings (or gods of the four directions of space, as they are also called) up to the gods who control the creations of others. The plane of archetypal form comprises altogether sixteen sub-planes, from the heaven of the gods belonging to the company of Brahma, up to and including the five 'pure abodes' which are inhabited by Non-Returners, i.e. those great spiritual beings who have developed transcendental insight to such an extent as to break the five fetters binding them to the plane of sensuous desire, so that they will no more be reborn there. The third plane, the plane of no archetypal form, comprises four sub-planes, all of which are inhabited by Brahmas, a class of spiritual beings superior even to the gods (though sometimes spoken of as such).

Much could be said about these three planes of conditioned existence. All that concerns us at the moment is the fact that on the planes of archetypal form there is no such thing as sexual dimorphism, i.e. no separation into male and female, the inhabitants of these planes all being what we would call, from the human point of view, androgynous. Sexual dimorphism, or separation into male and female, is found only on the plane of sensuous desire, including of course the human world. Since spiritual life consists, in objective or cosmological terms, in a progression from lower to higher planes and worlds, spiritual life also consists in a progression from a state of biological and psychological sexual dimorphism to a state of spiritual androgyny. Moreover, since a state of sexual dimorphism is a state of polarization, tension, and projection, it is also a state of discontent. The state of spiritual androgyny, on the contrary, is a state of harmony, relaxation, and content. Observance of the

Third Precept, therefore, does not consist simply in abstention from the various well-known forms of sexual misconduct, but also, and more importantly, in the experience of Contentment, the 'vertical' as distinct from the 'horizontal' counterpart of such abstention.

In meditation the state of sexual dimorphism is transcended. In meditation one ceases, for the time being, to be either male or female. This is because in meditation, in the sense of *samathabhavana* or 'development of calm', one progresses through the *dhyanas* or states of higher consciousness, as they may be called, and these states of higher consciousness are the subjective, psychological counterparts of the different sub-planes of the planes of archetypal form and no archetypal form. While meditating, in the sense of actually experiencing the *dhyanas*, one is therefore a deva or Brahma. In terms of the Western spiritual tradition, one is an angel and leading an angelic life – angels of course being by nature androgynous. It is thus no accident of language that the Sanskrit word for what we call celibacy or, more correctly, chastity, is *brahmacarya* (Pali *brahmacariya*), which literally means faring, practising, or living like Brahma, i.e. not merely abstaining from sexual activity but transcending the sexual dimorphism on which sexual activity and sexual desire are based.

This is why Vajraloka, our meditation and retreat centre in North Wales, is dedicated not only to meditation (*dhyana*) but also to celibacy (*brahmacarya*). Meditation and celibacy go together: they mutually reinforce each other. For the same reason, we encourage single-sex situations of every kind. This is not simply in order to curtail the opportunities for sexual misconduct, but also, more positively, to give both men and women some respite from the tensions of sexual polarization and to provide them with an opportunity of transcending, for a few moments, the state of sexual polarization, and being simply a human being and – to some extent – a true individual. For those who wish to develop as individuals, and to progress on the path to Enlightenment, meditation and all kinds of single-sex situations are, in the absence of transcendental insight, absolutely indispensable.

From all this it also follows not only that abstention from sexual misconduct is not enough, not only that one must experience contentment, but that one should not think of oneself as being either a man or a woman in any absolute or exclusive sense. After all, according to traditional Buddhist teaching, in the course of the beginningless series of one's existences one has been both a man and a woman many times. One has even, perhaps, been a god – an androgynous being. Within a perspective of this kind it would seem quite ridiculous to think and to feel that, just because one happened to be a man or a woman in this existence, one was a man or a woman for ever and ever, world without end, amen.

To the extent that one ceases to think of oneself as being a man or a woman in any absolute and exclusive sense, to that extent one will cease to speak and act as though one was a man and nothing but a man, or a woman and nothing but a woman – that is to say, one will cease to behave in that sexually ultra-polarized fashion which for Buddhism is exemplified by the figures of the male and female *asuras*. Male *asuras* are fierce, aggressive and very ugly, rather like the orcs in *The Lord of the Rings*. The female *asuras* are voluptuous, seductive, and very beautiful, and eat any human males who are so unfortunate as to fall into their clutches. What the male *asuras* do to human females we are not told, though no doubt it can be imagined. Members of the Western Buddhist Order have no wish to resemble *asuras* of either sex.

This does not mean that sexual differences can be simply 'ironed out' or ignored, or that it is possible to pretend that they do not exist. A feeble and colourless unisexuality, which merely seeks to negate sexual differences on their own level, is not to be confused with the ideal of spiritual androgyny. A castrate is not an angel, certain representations of angels in Christian art notwithstanding. Here as elsewhere in the spiritual life what is needed is not negation but transformation, not evasion but progression. So far as the Third Precept is concerned, especially in its positive formulation as Contentment, this progression is from an absolute identification with one psychophysical sex to a relative and provisional identification with it, and from a relative and provisional identification with it to no identification at all. If we can only see this, whether with or without the help of traditional Buddhist cosmology, we shall understand the Third Precept more deeply, and because we understand it more deeply we shall observe it with greater confidence. Theory and practice will both be clear.

They will be clear as crystal, for the Third Precept is a pillar of crystal. It is a pillar of crystal because crystal is pure, transparent, and brilliant, and either colourless or only slightly tinged with pink or blue.

The Fourth Precept
The Principle of Abstention from False Speech; or Truthfulness

Before we deal with this Precept let me make a few general remarks about the four speech precepts collectively. The first thing that strikes us is that there should be four of them at all. Even though speech is a 'door' or 'avenue' in its own right, and as such of equal importance with body and mind, it is rather as though there should be four separate precepts for four different kinds of killing, or four separate precepts for as many different ways of taking what is not given. Obviously, speech is of great importance. As the principal vehicle of communication between man and man it plays a social role in human development, while as the principal medium for that system of expression which we call language it is, with language itself, one of the distinguishing characteristics of man as compared with other animals.

For Buddhism speech is important because it occupies an intermediate position between body and mind, or between action and thought, being neither so gross as the one nor so subtle as the other. It is because it occupies this intermediate position that it is so important to control speech – and also why it is so difficult to control it. It is important to control speech because speech is, in a sense, a form of action, i.e. a form of overt action, and as such takes its place in the external world and has consequences there both for oneself and for others. As the *Dhammapada* says with regard to one particular form of unskilful speech:

Do not speak roughly to anyone: those thus spoken to will answer back. (Because) angry talk is extremely painful (to bear) you will experience retribution.[19]

It is difficult to control speech because speech is, in a sense, not just thought indeed but, for the speaker himself, so close to thought (after all, speech is only vocalized thought) that he often has difficulty in realizing that what he says is capable of producing tangible effects in the outside world and that speech ought, therefore, to be controlled. No doubt it is for this reason that in the formula of the Ten Precepts no fewer than four precepts out of ten are concerned with speech, whereas in the formula of the Noble Eightfold Path only one 'member' out of eight is so concerned (though that member is, of course, divided into four).

Buddhist tradition also points out that speech can be controlled by paying systematic attention to what comes out of this 'door', as well as by observing periods of complete silence from time to time. (Vows of perpetual silence are not permitted in Buddhism, as hindering the propagation of the Dharma.)

For the vast majority of people the stream of speech is so constant and so uninterrupted, and so much under the influence of unskilful mental factors, many of them unconscious, that all four speech precepts are likely to be broken many times a day, every day of the week. Speech is therefore something about which all Buddhists are expected to be particularly careful.

'Abstention from False Speech' can be practised without practising 'Truthfulness' only by abstaining from speech itself altogether. But abstention from false speech is by no means enough. Like all the other Precepts, the Fourth Precept must be observed in its positive form as well as in its negative form. When one says that speech is important because it is the principal vehicle of communication between man and man one is really speaking of truthful speech, and of truthful speech only.

Untruthful speech cannot be a vehicle of communication, so that in any human society in which untruthful speech predominates communication will break down. Without truthful speech there can be no civilization and culture; indeed, there can be no spiritual life and no Spiritual Community. Without truthfulness society itself cannot exist, so that whoever is guilty of false speech in fact undermines the foundations of society. A liar is an anti-social element – especially in a court of justice.

This is why telling lies in a court of justice, when one has been called upon to speak the truth, is for Buddhism the paradigmatic form of false speech, just as speaking the truth in those circumstances is the paradigmatic form of truthfulness – as we saw in the case of the Buddha's teaching to Cunda the silversmith about the threefold cleansing. The bearing of false witness is such a terrible offence because it renders the administration of justice impossible, and if justice cannot be administered society ceases to be a moral order, the rule of right being replaced by the rule of might.

Bearing false witness is not the only form of false speech that undermines the foundations of society. George Orwell's Newspeak – indeed, any kind of insincere jargon – can have the same devastating effect. Confucius, when asked what he would put first if entrusted with the administration of a state, replied 'The rectification of terms'.[20] In similar vein, what Nietzsche appreciated most about Zarathustra (i.e. the real Zarathustra, not the product of his own philosophico-poetic imagination) was that his teaching upheld truthfulness as the supreme virtue. 'To tell the truth and *to shoot well with arrows*: that is Persian virtue',[21] he tells us, as though these two things comprised both the law and the prophets.

The *Dhammapada* says much the same thing, though in negative rather than positive terms, when it declares:

> There is no evil that cannot be done by a lying person, who has transgressed one precept, and who holds in contempt the world beyond.[22]

As if to say that a man who tells lies, and who does not recognize the existence of a higher world of moral and spiritual values, is capable of breaking every other precept.

One of the simplest, yet most important, forms of abstention from false speech and cultivation of truthfulness is that of factual accuracy. This consists in telling what one has seen, for example, or what one has heard, with scrupulous fidelity to the facts as they actually occurred, neither adding nor subtracting anything, nor exaggerating or minimizing anything, and without failing to recount any relevant circumstances. The observance of the Fourth Precept even in this limited sense is extremely difficult, and there is no doubt that we need to school ourselves in factual accuracy much more rigorously if we are to have any hope of observing this Precept in its subtle, refined, and advanced forms. On numerous occasions I have been both astonished and dismayed at the careless manner in which some of my own remarks have been reported, or verbal messages delivered, even by those from whom I had reason to expect greater scrupulousness in this regard.

Such carelessness can be not only a source of general uncertainty and confusion but also of serious misunderstanding between one person and another. In repeating to one person what has been said by another one cannot, therefore, take too much trouble to ensure that one repeats what was said, and repeats it in such a way as to convey both the spirit and the letter of the other person's utterance, since otherwise a breach of the Fourth Precept will very likely become a breach of the Seventh as well.

There are many other points that could be made in connection with the Fourth Precept, but most of them are points I have already made on other occasions. Before telling you of which precious stone or precious metal the pillar of the Fourth Precept is made I shall, therefore, make a point that I have never made before. Though it does not concern one's personal observance of the Fourth Precept it is, nonetheless, a point of very great importance.

When we speak the truth we do, of course, expect to be believed, since otherwise no communication can take place. Similarly, we should believe others when *they* speak the truth. Next to killing a man, perhaps the worst possible thing you can do to him – and this is the point I want to make – is not to believe him when he is speaking the truth. Not to believe him when he is speaking the truth negates his identity as a social being and disrupts human solidarity. Such disbelief is, in fact, an act of violence.

It is not enough, therefore, that we should speak the truth: we should also believe others when they speak it – especially within the Spiritual Community. This means that we shall have to develop sufficient awareness and sensitivity to tell when another person really is speaking the truth, since otherwise we may unintentionally do them a great wrong.

The Fourth Precept is a pillar of pearl, if you can imagine such a thing. It is a pillar of pearl because in order to find pearls one must dive into the depths of the ocean. Similarly, one has to dive very deep to discover the truth, even in the most obvious factual sense, and until one has discovered it one can hardly speak it.

The Fifth Precept
The Principle of Abstention from Harsh Speech; or Kindly Speech

Much of what has been said with regard to the deeper significance of the four previous precepts, especially the last one, can be applied, *mutatis mutandis*, to the remaining three speech precepts. Hence it will not be necessary for us to deal with these precepts at anything like the same length as the Fourth Precept. I shall confine myself to making a few points which, though minor in relation to the great themes already discussed, are nevertheless of some practical importance.

With regard to the negative form of the Fifth Precept, it is necessary to abstain not only from harsh speech in its cruder and more obvious forms, but also from indulgence in coarse, indecent, and obscene language of every kind. Such language has become extremely common in recent decades, the use of four-letter words in particular now being variously regarded as a sign of rugged masculinity, of freedom from convention, and of artistic integrity, instead of what in truth it is: a sign of emotional immaturity, impoverished imagination, and limited vocabulary.

Speaking personally, I think I can say that with the possible exception of two or three occasions on which I quoted remarks made by other people, I have not used bad language even once in my life. Even as a boy, the few mild expletives I heard within the family circle pained and disgusted me, and when I was still quite young I realized that for me the use of such language was, in fact, an impossibility. Coarse, indecent, and obscene language, it seemed to me even then, was the expression of strongly negative emotional states and quite literally poisoned the atmosphere.

Perhaps I should make it clear that I regard as being included in language of this sort all those unpleasant and offensive expressions by which women are reduced, in the mouths of some men, to their lowest common sexual denominator. Such expressions are a form of Harsh Speech, and Buddhists are expected to eschew them no less than their various unlovely brethren.

Just as Harsh Speech poisons the atmosphere, so Kindly Speech, the positive counterpart of Abstention from Harsh Speech, purifies and invigorates it. Kindly Speech is like the warm rays of the rising sun, that cause leaves to expand and flowers to open. People often do not realize how positive an effect can be produced by a few friendly words. Kindly Speech, or Affectionate Speech, as we can also call it, should be habitual to us, not just something we keep for use in emergencies, or for special occasions, or special people.

One of the principal forms of Kindly Speech is what is known in Buddhism as Rejoicing in Merits, and I am glad to say that within the FWBO this particular expression of emotional positivity has become more and more popular in recent years. Among the subordinate forms of Kindly Speech are gentle speech, courteous speech, and even polite speech, which although of minor importance are not so unimportant that we can afford to neglect them. Whether inside or outside the FWBO, they all help to create an atmosphere of positivity within which spiritual friendship can develop and the spiritual life can be led.

The Fifth Precept is a pillar of amber, which is neither a precious stone nor a precious metal, but a translucent organic substance that takes a fine polish. In colour amber is a deep, warm, reddish yellow, rather like honey, and has a kind of fiery gleam in its depths. Moreover, by friction amber becomes strongly electric, and capable of attracting other bodies.

The Sixth Precept
The Principle of Abstention from Frivolous Speech; or Meaningful Speech

In a passage that occurs more than once in the Pali scriptures the Buddha lists thirty-two kinds of frivolous, idle, useless, or meaningless talk in which his followers should not indulge. Two thousand five hundred years later there are – thanks to radio, television, and the press – at least thirty-two thousand kinds of such talk, and it is more important than ever that we should not lose sight of the principle that underlies lists of this sort, i.e. the principle of Abstention from Frivolous Speech or, in terms of its positive formulation, of Meaningful Speech.

Speech can be truly meaningful only when life is meaningful, and life can be meaningful only when we have a definite purpose and a definite goal. For a Buddhist, this goal is Enlightenment, which means that for a Buddhist meaningful speech is speech about the Dharma, for it is the Dharma that is the means to Enlightenment. Indeed, it is not so much that the Dharma is the means to Enlightenment, in its own right as it were, as that 'the Dharma' is the collective designation for all those doctrines and methods, insights and observances, that actually help us to move in the direction of the Transcendental. The Dharma is whatever helps us to develop as individuals, though not individualistically, since true individual development comprises an other-regarding as well as a self-regarding aspect.

Meaningful Speech is therefore not speech about the Dharma in any merely formal sense, much less still a matter of 'pious talk' (as more than one eminent translator has rendered the Pali term '*dhamma-katha*'), but talk about the means to Enlightenment, or whatever helps us to develop as individuals. One can say more than that. Meaningful Speech is itself a means to Enlightenment inasmuch as it is a communication in depth between two or more people who are committed to the Ideal of Enlightenment, or who have gone for Refuge.

That one should engage in Meaningful Speech to the entire exclusion of Frivolous Speech does not, however, mean that one should drag in the subject of Buddhism on each and every occasion, in season and out, like the man in one of G.K. Chesterton's stories who, regardless of what the other person started talking about, always contrived to bring the conversation round to the subject of the Roman Catholic Church. If one is oneself committed to the Ideal of Enlightenment the fact of that commitment will emerge quite naturally in the course of conversation, and one's speech will become Meaningful Speech without any special effort. This will happen, though, only if one remains constantly aware of one's commitment, or of the overall purpose of one's existence, and constantly aware of the direction in which the conversation is moving, as well as of the atmosphere of the gathering. Frivolous Speech is liable to erupt whenever two or three people meet, and unless one is unremittingly vigilant the pure silver of Meaningful Speech will soon be tarnished by the breath of one or more of its thirty-two – or thirty-two thousand – noxious forms.

Thus Meaningful Speech is a pillar of silver. It is a pillar of silver not only because it is liable to tarnish unless burnished by insight, but because, like gold, it is malleable and ductile, and capable of taking on as many different forms as the Dharma. Like gold too, it is a common medium of exchange, the exchange in this case being the spiritual and existential exchange that takes place in the course of genuinely human communication.

The Seventh Precept
The Principle of Abstention from Slanderous Speech; or Harmonious Speech

The malicious speech from which the Seventh Precept requires us to abstain is malicious in a special way, so that the harmonious speech which constitutes the positive counterpart of such abstention is harmonious in a special way. Malice is, of course, enmity of heart, hatred, or ill will, and malicious speech in the most general sense is speech that proceeds from, or is dictated by, unskilful mental states of that kind. In the context of the Seventh Precept, however, the object of the enmity, hatred, or ill will from which malicious speech proceeds, or by which it is dictated, is the state of unity, concord, or amity existing between two or more people. Thus malicious speech is speech which brings about – and is intended to bring about – disunity, discord, and enmity. For this reason *pisunavaca* is sometimes translated not as malicious speech but as 'slanderous speech' or 'backbiting'.

The real nature of the Principle of Abstention from Malicious Speech, or Harmonious Speech, is well brought out in the Buddha's teaching to Cunda the silversmith, reference to which has already been made. Abandoning slanderous speech and abstaining therefrom, the Buddha says of one who observes this Precept: 'When he hears something at one place he does not proclaim it elsewhere to bring about a quarrel between the parties; what he has heard here he does not report there to bring about a quarrel between the parties.' Quarrels, and hence disunity, often begin with a third party deliberately stirring up trouble by telling two people, or two groups of people, what each is supposed to have said about the other in their absence. Sometimes this is a pure invention, but more often it is something which actually was said but which has been taken out of context, or garbled in the telling. The person observing the Seventh Precept abstains from all such crooked behaviour. 'Thus he brings together the discordant, restores harmony.' In other words, even when people have fallen out of their own accord, so to speak, harmony can be restored if others do not make matters worse with their tale-bearing. Harmony is his delight, he exults in harmony, he is passionately fond of harmony. The Buddha's language here is very strong. One who observes the Seventh Precept does not merely abstain from malicious speech: he takes a positive delight in harmony, and it is because of this that 'he utters speech which makes for harmony', as when one tells somebody what good things a friend has said about him, or how he has defended him against criticism. From this it is evident that the positive counterpart of Abstention from Malicious Speech is not so much Harmonious Speech as Harmonizing Speech, i.e. speech which transforms discord into harmony and raises the harmony that already exists between people to an even higher level. The applicability of this to the Spiritual Community should be obvious.

The Seventh Precept is a pillar of opal. It is a pillar of opal, or of what is called precious or noble opal, because opal brings all the different colours of the rainbow together in a single gem, just as the Principle of Abstention from Malicious Speech, or of Harmonious– or Harmonizing – Speech brings people of many different kinds together in a single society or community.

The Eighth Precept
The Principle of Abstention from Covetousness; or Tranquillity

With the Eighth Precept we pass from the precepts governing speech to the precepts governing mind. We also pass from the seven precepts that make up *sila* or ethics in the narrower sense to the three precepts that, together with the seven previous precepts, make up *sila* or ethics in the broader sense. Since the three precepts governing mind are concerned not so much with bodily and vocal behaviour as with the inner attitudes of which that behaviour is the outward expression, they are obviously of the utmost importance. Unfortunately, however, we shall have to deal with the first two of them, at least, no less briefly than with the last three speech precepts. The reason for this is that, as we shall see (and as we indeed saw in connection with the Ten Precepts and Other Ethical Formulae), the Eighth and Ninth Precepts are concerned with that part of mental conduct which comprises the noble group of *samadhi* or concentration and meditation, even as the Tenth Precept is that part of it which is concerned with the noble group of wisdom, and with a subject as vast as that of concentration and meditation it is not possible for us to deal on this occasion. It will be enough if I can establish a few connections.

In its negative form the Eighth Precept consists in Abstention from Covetousness, the Pali word here rendered as 'covetousness' being *abhijjha*. We can arrive at some understanding of the deeper significance of this term not only by analysing the meaning of the term itself but also by examining three other important terms with which it is approximately synonymous. Strange as it may seem at first sight, the second part of the word *abhijjha* is from *jhayati* (Sanskrit *dhyayati*), meaning 'to meditate, contemplate, think upon, brood over: search for, hunt after', from which the word *jhana* (Sanskrit *dhyana*) is also derived. *Abhi* is a prefix meaning 'very much, greatly'. *Abhijjha* thus signifies a mental state of intense thinking upon, or brooding over, something by which we are attracted, or which we desire, i.e. it signifies a mental state of covetousness.

The three terms which are approximately synonymous with *abhijjha* are *lobha*, *tanha* (Sanskrit *trsna*), and *raga*. *Lobha* means 'greed, lust, longing, desire', and is cognate with the Latin *libido*, as well as with the German *Lieb* and English love. *Tanha* means 'thirst', and like the English words thirst and drought is ultimately from a root meaning dryness, while *raga* (literally colour, hue, dye), has the meaning of 'excitement, passion'.

From the nature of these terms we can see, in a general way, what kind of mental state it is with which the Principle of Abstention from Covetousness is concerned. It is a state, essentially, in which the self or ego reaches out towards the non-self or non-ego with a view to appropriating and even incorporating it, thus filling the yawning pit of its own inner poverty and emptiness. Since it is not really possible to appropriate an external object in this way, the state of covetousness is therefore also a state of perpetual frustration. For this reason the term *abhijjha* is often combined, in the Pali scriptures, with the term *domanassa* or 'distress, dejectedness, melancholy, grief'. In other words, the Principle of Abstention from Covetousness is concerned with that state of general, existential polarization between coveting subject and coveted object of which the sexual polarization referred to in connection with the Third Precept is only a particular – though perhaps the most conspicuous – example.

For the positive counterpart of Abstention from Covetousness there is no wholly suitable term. In the context of the Ten Positive Precepts we speak of 'abandoning covetousness for generosity', but besides being the positive counterpart of Abstention from Taking the Not-Given, the term generosity is not really radical enough. Just as covetousness represents the mental state on account of which one takes what is not given, so the positive counterpart of Abstention from Covetousness should represent the mental state on account of which one practises generosity. Such a state could, of course, be spoken of as a state of depolarization, except that the expression is rather abstract, and in any case negative in form. It could also be spoken of as a state of detachment, except that that too is negative, or as one of contentment, had that term not already been used as the positive counterpart of Abstention from Sexual Misconduct. Perhaps it will be best to speak of the positive counterpart of Abstention from Covetousness as Tranquillity.

The connection between the Eighth Precept and meditation – indeed, between all the three mind precepts and meditation – should be obvious. Meditation is the subjective or direct method of raising the level of consciousness, as distinct from Right Livelihood, or Hatha Yoga, or *kalyana mitrata*, which are objective or indirect ways of raising it. Since consciousness is made up of various mental states, the fact that meditation is the direct means of raising the level of consciousness does not mean that there is a single, as it were generic form of meditation which does this. Meditation has a number of specific forms, each one of which raises the general level of consciousness by working on a particular unskilful mental state. Covetousness being a reaching out of the self or ego towards the non-self or non-ego, that form of meditation will be able to eradicate covetousness which has the effect of checking this tendency and enabling one to realize its futility.

There are several meditations of this kind. Among them are the Recollection of Death, the Recollection of Impurity (i.e. the ten 'corpse meditations'), and the Recollection of the Six Elements, with all of which practices most Order members are well acquainted. Indeed, in recent years it has become a tradition for Mitras to engage in an intensive practice of the Recollection of the Six Elements during the weeks immediately preceding 'ordination' or Going for Refuge. In this way they not only experience the 'death' that precedes spiritual 'rebirth' as an Order member, but also lay the foundation for a thoroughgoing practice of the Principle of Abstention from Covetousness, or Tranquillity.

The Eighth Precept is a pillar of emerald. It is a pillar of emerald because the deep rich green of the emerald is a 'cool' rather than a 'hot' colour and as such fittingly stands for a state in which the fever of covetousness has cooled down. Green is also the colour of vegetation, the calming and soothing effect of which on the mind is well known.

The Ninth Precept
The Principle of Abstention from Hatred; or Compassion

As in the case of *abhijjha*, we can arrive at a deeper understanding of the term rendered by 'Hatred' not only by analysing the meaning of the term itself but also by examining other terms with which it is approximately synonymous. *Vyapada* (or *byapada*) means 'making bad, doing harm; desire to injure, malevolence, ill-will', and it is cognate with *vyadhi* meaning 'sickness, malady, illness, disease', as well as with *vyadha* or huntsman. Thus it is clear that the general sense of the word is that of wishing evil. The terms that are closest to *vyapada* in meaning are *dosa* (Sanskrit *dvesa*), *kodha* (Sanskrit *krodha*), and *vera* (Sanskrit *vaira*). *Dosa* is 'anger, ill-will, evil intention, wickedness, corruption, malice, hatred', while *kodha* is simply anger and *vera* enmity.

The real nature of the unskilful mental state with which the Ninth Precept is concerned emerges, however, only when we are able to see the connection between 'Hatred' and 'Covetousness'. If covetousness is the state in which the self or ego reaches out towards the non-self or non-ego with a view to appropriating or even incorporating it, hatred is the state that arises when that movement of reaching out is checked, hindered, or obstructed either by the non-self or non-ego itself or by some other factor or party. Thus if covetousness is the primary psychological formation, hatred is the secondary one. It is the murderous wish to do the utmost possible harm and damage to whatever interposes itself between coveting subject and coveted object.

As for the positive counterpart of the Principle of Abstention from Hatred, this is not Love, as one might have thought, but Compassion. The term Love has, of course, already been used as the positive counterpart of Abstention from Killing; but the real reason why it is Compassion rather than Love is that the positive counterpart of Abstention from Hatred is to be found in the Bodhisattva Ideal. According to the *Upali-pariprccha* or 'Questions of (the Arhant) Upali', a Mahayana sutra of the Ratnakuta class, for a Bodhisattva to break precepts out of desire (= covetousness) is a minor offence, even if he does so for innumerable *kalpas*, whereas for him to break precepts out of anger (= hatred) even once is a very serious offence. The reason for this is that 'a Bodhisattva who breaks precepts out of desire [still] holds sentient beings in his embrace, whereas a Bodhisattva who breaks precepts out of hatred forsakes sentient beings altogether.'[23] Here as elsewhere, of course, the Mahayana is not saying that the breaking of precepts out of desire doesn't matter, but saying – in its own hyperbolical way – that for the Bodhisattva it is of supreme importance that he should not, under any circumstances, forsake sentient beings, which of course he does do when he breaks precepts out of hatred. Hatred and Compassion are mutually exclusive. Thus 'Compassion' rather than 'Love' is the positive counterpart of Abstention from Hatred.

The forms of meditation which have the effect of checking the hatred which arises when covetousness is hindered or obstructed are the four Brahma Viharas, i.e. the systematic cultivation (*bhavana*) of the positive mental states of love, compassion, sympathetic joy, and equanimity, as well as such practices as Rejoicing in Merits and the Sevenfold Puja. Once hatred has been eradicated, one can then proceed to deal with the underlying state of covetousness that makes hatred possible.

The Ninth Precept is a pillar of ruby. It is a pillar of ruby because the typical ruby is a deep clear red, and red is not only the colour of love and compassion but also, more literally, the colour of blood – of that blood which the Bodhisattva is willing to shed, throughout hundreds of lives, for the benefit of all living beings.

The Tenth Precept
The Principle of Abstention from False Views; or Wisdom

In relation to the importance of its subject-matter, the length at which we shall be dealing with the Tenth Precept will mean that even less justice will be done to the Principle of Abstention from False Views, or Wisdom, than was done to the subject-matter of the last two Precepts. It will be possible to do little more, in fact, than indicate what is meant by false views and how they are to be abandoned, though for the purposes of this paper that will be enough. The Pali term for which 'false views' is the generally accepted rendering is *miccha-ditthi* or *miccha-dasana* (Sanskrit *mithya-drsti*, *mithya-darsana*). *Miccha* means simply 'wrong' or 'false', while *ditthi* means 'view, belief, dogma, theory, esp. false theory, groundless or unfounded opinion.'

Thus *miccha-ditthi* or *miccha-dasana* means in the first place a wrong or false view, in the sense of a wrong or false way of seeing things, and in the second place a wrong or false view as expressed more or less systematically in intellectual terms in the form of a doctrine.

117

What makes the view, or the doctrine, wrong or false is the fact that it is an expression, not to say a rationalization, of a mental state contaminated by covetousness and hatred, as well as by delusion (*moha*), the cognitive counterpart of covetousness. Only that view is *samyak* (Pali *samma*) or right, true, or perfect, which is the expression of a mental state uncontaminated by covetousness, hatred, and delusion, i.e. which is the expression of an Enlightened consciousness which sees things as they really are, though it is not right simply in the sense of being the opposite of wrong or false view.

Right view is also a non-view. It is a non-view in the sense that it is not held with the same pertinacity, or the same conviction of its absolute rightness, that false views are usually held (such pertinacity and conviction are themselves unskilful mental states), but as it were provisionally and tentatively as a means to the attainment of Enlightenment and not as an end in itself. The Buddha indeed once declared: 'The Tathagata has no views.' Though seeing things as they really are, he has a 'critical' awareness of the impossibility of giving full and final expression to his vision in fixed conceptual terms. It is for this reason that, although he teaches the Dharma, he teaches it 'as a Raft', i.e. as something to be left behind once the Other Shore has been reached.

In his teaching to Cunda the silversmith the Buddha enumerates some four or five false views of a very simple and basic kind. (The corresponding right views, which are enumerated later in the sutta, form part of the passage quoted in connection with the canonical sources of the Ten Precepts.) Speaking of the one whose mind is defiled, the Buddha says:

> Also he has wrong view, he is perverse in outlook, holding: There is no gift, no offering, no sacrifice; there is no fruit or ripening of deeds well done or ill done; the world is not, the world beyond is not; there is no mother, no father, no beings supernaturally born; there are no recluses or brahmins in the world who have gone right, who fare rightly, men who by their own comprehension have realized this world and the world beyond, and thus declare.[24]

In other words, such a person holds, in effect, that actions do not have consequences and that there is no difference, therefore, between skilful and unskilful actions; that there are no higher spiritual values, and no such thing as a distinctively human, morally-based social order; that in the scale of existence there are no living beings higher than sexually dimorphous man, as we at present know him, and no such thing as the spiritual life and no possibility of anyone personally realizing the ultimate truth of things. These false views are simple and basic in the sense that they deny, in the crudest and bluntest fashion, the possibility of even the most rudimentary form of moral and spiritual life and render the observance of the Ten Precepts unnecessary.

False views of a more subtle and sophisticated kind, which preclude the possibility of more advanced forms of spiritual life and experience by absolutizing, rather than denying, its more elementary forms, are to be found in the *Brahmajala-sutta*, the first of the thirty-two discourses of the *Digha-Nikaya*. That the *Brahmajala-sutta* or 'Perfect Net' discourse should be the first discourse of the *Digha-Nikaya*, and thus the first discourse of the entire Tripitaka, is no less significant than that the Book of Genesis should be the first book of the Bible.

In this sutta the Buddha enumerates and systematically analyses a total of sixty-four false views, some of which are very subtle and sophisticated indeed. These views between them comprehend all possible false views, and are thus the 'Perfect Net' in which all these 'recluses and brahmins' (i.e. philosophers and theologians) who adhere to false views are caught. Whether subtle and sophisticated, however, or simple and basic, all false views must be abandoned before Enlightenment can be attained.

Since false views are the precipitates and crystallizations of unskilful mental states, the most effective way of abandoning false views is by eradicating the unskilful mental states by which they are produced. This is best done with the help of meditation. It is, indeed, by preventing and eradicating unskilful mental states, and originating and developing skilful ones, that meditation raises the level of consciousness, the *dhyanas* or so-called 'states of higher consciousness' being in fact nothing but an uninterrupted flow of skilful mental states of increasing purity and intensity.

As we have already seen, covetousness can be eradicated with the help of the Recollection of Death, the Recollection of Impurity, and the Recollection of the Six Elements, and hatred with the help of the four Brahma Viharas, as well as by such practices as Rejoicing in Merits and the Sevenfold Puja. Similarly, delusion, which is in a sense the ultimate source not only of all false views but also of covetousness and hatred themselves, can be eradicated with the help of such practices as the Mindfulness of Breathing, the Recollection of the Six Elements, and the contemplation of the Twelve (or the Twenty-Four) Nidanas, as well as by concentrated reflection on such doctrinal formulae as the three characteristics of conditioned existence and the four kinds of *sunyata* or voidness.

False views can also be abandoned with the help of Dharma study of the traditional type, and by openhearted discussion with those members of the

Spiritual Community whose emotional positivity and intellectual clarity are superior to one's own.

Whatever the means employed, the more that false views are genuinely and radically abandoned, the more there shines forth what is variously termed Insight, or Perfect Vision, or Wisdom; and conversely the more Insight, or Perfect Vision, or Wisdom shines forth, the more false views are abandoned. When false views have been entirely abandoned, what shines forth in all its glory is Wisdom in its fullness, and it is this Wisdom that is the positive counterpart of Abstention from False Views. That it is the positive counterpart of Abstention from False Views does not mean that it consists simply in holding right views rather than wrong views. Wisdom holds no views, not even right views, though it may make use of right views for the communication of the Dharma.

In the world of today Wisdom is a rare and precious thing, and much could be said about the false views that assail us from every side, particularly as a result of the dominance of the media of so called mass-communication. But it is time for us to see of what kind of precious stone the tenth and last pillar is made. Before we do this I would like to make it clear that if we want even to begin to observe the Tenth Precept, under the present very difficult circumstances, we must do at least three things. (a) We must become more acutely aware of the extent to which our thinking, and the expression we give our thinking, is influenced by the false views by which we have been surrounded since birth. (b) We must realize not only that false views are the product of unskilful mental states but that, so long as they are not definitely abandoned, they actually reinforce the unskilful mental states which produce them, thus doubly obstructing the path to Enlightenment. (c) We must resolve that whenever we discuss personal spiritual difficulties, or issues concerning the Order and the Movement as a whole, and above all when we discuss the Dharma itself, we should do so in terms of Right Views – if possible in terms of Wisdom – and *not* in terms of any of the false views which are currently fashionable in the outside world.

We should discuss Buddhism in the language of Buddhism. If after careful study we come to the conclusion that the language of Blake, or of Heidegger, or of William Morris, to some extent coincides with the language of Buddhism, then that is a different matter, and we can feel free to communicate the Dharma in their language too if that seems the skilful and appropriate thing to do. But to try to communicate the Dharma in terms of a view, or a language, which explicitly or implicitly negates the very possibility of Wisdom can only result in confusion.

The Tenth Precept is a pillar of sapphire. It is a pillar of sapphire because sapphire is a deep, intense blue, and blue is the colour of the unclouded sky, with which Wisdom, the positive counterpart of Abstention from False Views, is often compared.

Conclusion

Now that we have seen of which precious stone the last pillar is made, we can see the Ten Precepts both in their collective majesty and in their individual beauty and splendour. We can see that the Ten Precepts are indeed the Ten Pillars of Buddhism, and that they comprise a pillar of diamond, a pillar of gold, a pillar of crystal, a pillar of pearl, a pillar of amber, a pillar of silver, a pillar of opal, a pillar of emerald, a pillar of ruby, and a pillar of sapphire. These ten pillars are the massy supports of the entire majestic edifice of the Dharma, and if some of you are disappointed that some of your favourite precious stone or precious metal does not enter into the composition of any of the pillars, let me remind you that although no mention has been made of them the pillars themselves all have bases and capitals, arches and archivolts, and that these too are made of precious substances of various kinds.

Indeed, though at the beginning of this paper I spoke not only of the Ten Precepts as the double row of pillars supporting the spacious dome of the Dharma edifice, but also of Meditation as the dome itself, and of Wisdom as the lofty spire that surmounts the dome, we have not seen of which precious substances the dome and the spire are made. From what has been said about the last three Precepts, however, it will be obvious that the dome– a double dome – must be made of something not unlike emerald and ruby, and the spire of something not unlike sapphire.

There has also been no mention of the people who resort to the majestic edifice of the Dharma, wandering among the precious pillars and gazing up through the precious dome into the precious spire – and beyond. As it should hardly be necessary for me to tell you, we are the people who resort to the edifice of the Dharma, and in fact we are standing in the midst of it at this very moment, together with all those who have gone, and do now go, and will in future go, for Refuge to the Buddha, the Dharma, and the Sangha. But once here, surrounded by the precious pillars, and surmounted by the precious dome and the precious spire, what use of the majestic edifice do we make? And here our architectural metaphor breaks down. It breaks down because we are ourselves the pillars, the dome, and the spire, at least potentially. The architectural metaphor has to be replaced by a biological metaphor, in fact by a botanical metaphor.

The Ten Precepts are not only ten pillars; they are ten petals, the ten petals of a magnificent flower, of which Meditation is the stamen, and Wisdom the seed or fruit. We ourselves are that flower, both individually and 'collectively', and we grow and we bloom not for our own sake only, but for the sake of all living beings. In other words, dropping all metaphors, we observe the Ten Precepts because – apart from Going for Refuge itself – there is hardly anything that would be of greater importance and hardly anything that would be of greater benefit to ourselves and others. For this reason there could hardly be a better way for us to celebrate the sixteenth anniversary of the Western Buddhist Order than by trying to see more clearly how profound is the significance, and how far-reaching the implications, of the Ten Precepts. The more faithfully we observe the Ten Precepts, the greater will be the likelihood of the Western Buddhist Order truly attaining its 'collective' majority as a Spiritual Community – whether this year itself or in five years' time.

Let us therefore resolve that in the days that lie ahead we shall do all we can to strengthen and sustain the Ten Pillars of Buddhism.

Notes

1   *Minor Anthologies of the Pali Canon* Part II. Translated by F.L. Woodward, Pali Text Society, London, 1948, p.130.

2   See Sangharakshita, *A Survey of Buddhism* (seventh edition), Windhorse, Glasgow, 1993, pp.159–72, 461–84.

3   Maha Sthavira Sangharakshita, 'Aspects of Buddhist Morality', *Studia Missionalia*, Rome, 1978, Vol.27, pp.159–80.

4   By 'united' I mean spiritually united, rather than bound by ties of mutual socio-economic dependence.

5   *Dialogues of the Buddha*, Part I. Translated from the Pali by T.W. Rhys Davids, Pali Text Society, reprinted London, 1956, p.179.

6   *The Collection of the Middle Length Sayings (Majjhima-Nikaya)* Vol.III. Translated by I.B. Horner, M.A., Pali Text Society, London, 1959, pp.97–8.

7   *The Book of the Gradual Sayings (Anguttara-Nikaya)* Vol.V. Translated by F.L. Woodward, M.A., Pali Text Society, reprinted London, 1972, pp.178-80.

8   *The Mahavastu* Volume II. Translated from the Buddhist Sanskrit by J.J. Jones, M.A., Pali Text Society, London, 1952, p.91ff.

9   *The Perfection of Wisdom in Eight Thousand Lines and Its Verse Summary.* Translated by Edward Conze, Bolinas, 1973, pp.200–01.

10 *The Teaching of Vimalakirti (Vimalakirtinirdesa).* From the French translation by Etienne Lamotte, Pali Text Society, London, 1976, p.20.

11 *Ibid*, p.40.

12 *Ibid*, p.214.

13 *The Sutra of Golden Light*, being a translation of the *Suvarnabhasottamasutra* by R.E. Emmerick, Pali Text Society, London, 1970, p.12.

14 Here the *'prati'* in *pratimoksa* would seem to be assimilated to pratyeka (= *prati* + *eka*), meaning 'for a single person, individual, personal', as in Pratyeka Buddha.

15 *The Book of the Gradual Sayings (Anguttara-Nikaya)* Vol.V. Translated by F.L. Woodward, M.A., Pali Text Society, reprinted London, 1972, p.186.

16 *The Collection of the Middle Length Sayings (Majjhima-Nikaya)* Vol.III. Translated by I.B. Horner, M.A., Pali Text Society, London, 1959, p.104.

17 *Dhammapada*, vv.129–30 (author's translation).

18 *The Path of Light*. Rendered from the *Bodhi-*

charyavatara of Santi-Deva: A Manual of Mahayana Buddhism, L.D. Barnett, reprinted London, 1959, pp.79–80.

19 *Dhammapada*, v. 133.

20 *Analects* Book XIII, Chapter III. *The Analects of The Conversations of Confucius with his Disciples and Certain Others*, as translated into English by William Edward Soothill, reprinted OUP, 1941, p.129. Confucius: *The Analects (Lun-yu)*. Translated with an Introduction by D.C. Lau, Penguin, reprinted Harmondsworth, 1982, p.118.

21 Quoted *Thus Spoke Zarathustra*. Translated with an Introduction by R.J. Hollingdale, Penguin, reprinted Harmondsworth, 1969, p.31.

22 *Dhammapada*, v.176.

23 *A Treasury of Mahayana Sutras. Selections from the Maharatnakuta Sutra*. Translated by the Buddhist Association of the United States, Garma C.C. Chang, general editor, Pennsylvania and London, 1983, p.270.

24 *The Book of the Gradual Sayings (Anguttara-Nikaya)* Vol.V, Pali Text Society, p.178.